Anonymous

The Lutheran Almanac, for the Year of Our Lord and Saviour Jesus Christ, 1875

Arranged according to the system of the German calendars, with valuable statsitical information

Anonymous

The Lutheran Almanac, for the Year of Our Lord and Saviour Jesus Christ, 1875
Arranged according to the system of the German calendars, with valuable statsitical information

ISBN/EAN: 9783337314538

Printed in Europe, USA, Canada, Australia, Japan

Cover: Foto ©Lupo / pixelio.de

More available books at **www.hansebooks.com**

THE

Lutheran Almanac,

FOR THE YEAR OF OUR LORD AND SAVIOUR JESUS CHRIST,

1875,

And, until the Fourth of July, the Ninety-Ninth Year
of the Independence of the United States.

ARRANGED ACCORDING TO THE SYSTEM OF THE GERMAN CALENDARS,

WITH VALUABLE STATISTICAL INFORMATION.

All the calculations of this Almanac are made to solar or apparent time,
to which add the equation of time when the Sun is slow, and
subtract it when fast, for mean or clock time.

BALTIMORE:

PUBLISHED BY T. NEWTON KURTZ,

PUBLISHER, BOOKSELLER AND STATIONER,

No. 151 W. Pratt Street, opposite the "Maltby House."

For Sale also at

THE LUTHERAN PUBLICATION HOUSE,

42 North Ninth Street, PHILADELPHIA.

1. ECLIPSES FOR THE YEAR 1875.

There will be Two Eclipses this Year—both of the Sun.

The first is a total Eclipse of the Sun, April 6th, 1 o'clock 25 min. in the morning; therefore invisible here; visible in Africa, Asia, and the Indian Ocean.

The second is an Annular Eclipse of the Sun, September 29th, 6 o'clock 10 min. in the morning. Visible. The Sun rises eclipsed, and ends at 7 o'clock 6 min. in the morning. At Boston the Eclipse will be Annular.

2. SIGNS OF THE ZODIAC.

♈ Aries, or ram.

♉ Taurus, or bull.

♊ Gemini, or twins.

♋ Cancer, or crab-fish.

♌ Leo, or lion.

♍ Virgo, or virgin.

♎ Libra, or balance.

♏ Scorpio, or scorpion.

♐ Sagittarius, or bowman.

♑ Capricornus, or goat.

♒ Aquarius, or waterman.

♓ Pisces, the fishes.

3. ASTRONOMICAL CHARACTERS EXPLAINED.

New Moon.

Full Moon.

☊ Moon's ascending Node, or Dragon's head.

☋ Moon's descending Node, or Dragon's tail.

First Quarter.

Last Quarter.

Moon's Ascension.

Moon's descension.

☽ Moon in Apogee—furthest from the earth.

☾ Moon in Perigee—nearest to the earth.

4. PLANETS AND ASPECTS.

♄ Saturn,

♁ Earth,

☉ Sun,

♂ Mars,

☾ Moon,

☿ Mercury,

♀ Venus,

♃ Jupiter,

♅ Herschel.

♂ Conjunction, or planets in the same longitude.

✳ Sextile, when they are 60 degrees apart.

▢ Quartile, when they are 90 degrees distant.

△ Trine, when they are 120 degrees distant.

☍ Opposition, when they are 180 degrees distant.

5. THE FOUR SEASONS OR CARDINAL POINTS.

Vernal Equinox—☉ Sun enters ♈—March 20, 2 o'clock, 26m., P. M.

Summer Solstice—☉ Sun enters ♋—June 21, 10 o'clock, 45m., A. M.

Autumnal Equinox—☉ Sun enters ♎—Sept. 23, 12 o'clock, 10m., A. M.

Winter Solstice—☉ Sun enters ♑—Dec'r 21, 6 o'clock, 35m., P. M.

Jupiter (♃) is called the governing Planet this year.

6. CHRONOLOGICAL CYCLES.

Dominical Letter.........C.	Epact................23	Roman Indiction.........3
Golden Number........14	Solar Cycle. 8	Julian Period.........6588

The Jewish Era commences September 30th, 1875, with 5636.
The Mohammedan Era commences February 17th, 1875, with 1292.

7. MOVABLE FESTIVALS OF THE CHURCH.

Septuagesima Sunday.........Jan.	24	Ascension or Holy Thursday, May	6
Quinquagesima Sunday.......Feb'y	7	Whit-Sunday........ .... "	16
Shrove Tuesday................ "	9	Trinity Sunday................ "	23
Ash Wednesday................ "	10	Corpus Christi.................. "	27
Palm Sunday..................Mar.	21	First Sunday in Advent......Nov.	28
Easter Sunday................ "	28	Sundays after Trinity are.... 26	

8. EMBER DAYS.

February 17......March 19......September 15......December 15.

9. ORIGIN OF EASTER.

Easter, derived from a Saxon word meaning *to rise*, is the name given to the festival which commemorates the resurrection of Jesus Christ from the dead. It is always held on the Sunday after the full moon which immediately succeeds the 21st day of March, the vernal equinox. The occurrence of Easter Sunday regulates all the *movable* feasts of the year. It cannot be earlier than the 22d of March, nor later than the 25th of April.

Easter was anciently called the *Great Day*, the *Feast of Feasts*, and the *Queen of Feasts*.

Table Showing the Day of the Month on which Easter will come in each Year, from 1875 to 1893.

1875, March 28.	1880, March 28.	1885, April 5.	1890, April 6.
1876, April 16.	1881, April 17.	1886, April 25.	1891, March 29.
1877, April 1.	1882, April 9.	1887, April 10.	1892, April 17.
1878, April 21.	1883, March 25.	1888, April 1.	1893, April 2.
1879, April 13.	1884, April 13.	1889, April 21.	

To Ascertain the Length of the Day and Night.

Double the time of the Sun's setting for the length of the day. Double the time of the Sun's rising for the length of the night.

BOOKS AND STATIONERY.

A large assortment of SCHOOL BOOKS, SUNDAY SCHOOL *Library* and *Reward* Books; Illustrated *Reward Cards* and *Tickets;* Sunday School Music Books; CHURCH MUSIC BOOKS; BLANK BOOKS of every description, PAPERS, ENVELOPES, and a *general assortment* of STATIONERY for sale— *wholesale and retail*—by

T. NEWTON KURTZ,
151 W. Pratt Street, Baltimore.

1st Month. JANUARY, 1875. 31 Days.

D. M.	D. W.	Moon South. H. M.	Moon Rises or Sets. H. M.	Moon's Place. S. D.	Aspect of Planets and other Miscellanies.	Sun Slow. M.	Sun Rises. H. M.	Sun Sets. H. M.
1	Fr.	*New Year.*		♎ 25	☽☌♃♂. ☽in apo.☋.	4	7 20	4 40
2	Sa.	8 18	1 49	♏ 7	♃ rises 12.36.	4	7 20	4 40

(1) Sun. aft. New Year.] Matt. 2. 13-23. I. Pet. 4. 12-19. [Day's l., 9h. 22m.

D. M.	D. W.	Moon South.	Moon Rises or Sets.	Moon's Place.	Aspect of Planets and other Miscellanies.	Sun Slow.	Sun Rises.	Sun Sets.
3	**S.**	9 6	2 59	♏ 19	♂ rises 12.40.	5	7 19	4 41
4	M.	9 54	4 19	♐ 2	☌☽♀. ♀ rises 4 46.	5	7 19	4 41
5	Tu.	10 36	5 10	♐ 16	Sirius south 11.32.	6	7 18	4 42
6	W.	*Epiphany.*		♑ 0	Orion south 10.38.	6	7 18	4 42
7	Th.	11 59	☽ sets.	♑ 14	7th. ☌☽☿. ♃r.12.18	7	7 17	4 43
8	Fr.	12 52	5 50	♑ 29	Neptune stationary.	7	7 17	4 43
9	Sa.	1 46	6 59	♒ 13	☌☽♄. ♄ sets 6.49.	7	7 16	4 44

(2) 1st Sun. after Epiph.] Luke 2. 41-52. Rom. 12. 1-6. [Day's l., 9h. 28m.

D. M.	D. W.	Moon South.	Moon Rises or Sets.	Moon's Place.	Aspect of Planets and other Miscellanies.	Sun Slow.	Sun Rises.	Sun Sets.
10	**S.**	2 36	8 8	♒ 28	♀ in Perihelion.	8	7 16	4 44
11	M.	3 24	9 22	♓ 13	♀ rises 4.28.	8	7 15	4 45
12	Tu.	4 12	10 36	♓ 27	Rigel south 9.34.	9	7 14	4 46
13	W.	*Spener b.* 1635.		♈ 12	♀ greatest brilliancy.	9	7 14	4 46
14	Th.	6 0	morn.	♈ 26	14th. ☊. 7* so. 8.0.	9	7 13	4 47
15	Fr.	6 48	12 55	♉ 10	☌☿☉ superior.	10	7 13	4 47
16	Sa.	7 32	2 5	♉ 23	♂ rises 12 26.	10	7 12	4 48

(3) 2d Sun. after Epiph.] John 2. 1-11. Rom. 12. 6-16. [Day's l., 9h. 38m.

D. M.	D. W.	Moon South.	Moon Rises or Sets.	Moon's Place.	Aspect of Planets and other Miscellanies.	Sun Slow.	Sun Rises.	Sun Sets.
17	**S.**	8 48	3 12	♊ 6	☽ in per. ♃ rises 11.59	11	7 11	4 49
18	M.	9 40	4 21	♊ 19	□ Neptune ☉.	11	7 11	4 49
19	Tu.	10 33	5 26	♋ 2	♀ rises 4.9.	11	7 10	4 50
20	W.	11 26	6 27	♋ 15	□♃☉. ☉ enters ♒.	11	7 9	4 51
21	Th.	morn.	☽rises.	♋ 27	21st. ☿ gr. hel. lat. s.	12	7 9	4 51
22	Fr.	12 16	5 55	♌ 9	♄ sets 6.8.	12	7 8	4 52
23	Sa.	12 56	6 46	♌ 21	♂ rises 12 18.	12	7 7	4 53

(4) Septuages'a Sun.] Matt. 20. 1-16. I. Cor. 9. 24-27. [Day's l., 9h. 48m.

D. M.	D. W.	Moon South.	Moon Rises or Sets.	Moon's Place.	Aspect of Planets and other Miscellanies.	Sun Slow.	Sun Rises.	Sun Sets.
24	**S.**	1 39	7 33	♍ 3	Spica rises 11.25.	12	7 6	4 54
25	M.	2 36	8 30	♍ 15	Sirius south 10.10.	13	7 5	4 55
26	Tu.	3 34	9 28	♍ 27	♀ rises 3 58.	13	7 4	4 56
27	W.	4 32	10 26	♎ 9	☌☿♄. Capella so. 8.28	13	7 3	4 57
28	Th.	5 31	11 25	♎ 21	☌☽♃. ♃ rises 11.21.	13	7 2	4 58
29	*Cath. v. B. b.* 1499.			♏ 3	29th. ☽ in apo. ☋	14	7 1	4 59
30	Sa	7 27	12 24	♏ 15	☌☽♂. ♂ rises 12 9.	14	7 0	5 0

(5) Sexages'a Sun.] Luke 8. 4-15. II. Cor. 11. 19-31. [Day's l., 10h. 2m.

D. M.	D. W.	Moon South.	Moon Rises or Sets.	Moon's Place.	Aspect of Planets and other Miscellanies.	Sun Slow.	Sun Rises.	Sun Sets.
31	**S.**	8 25	1 28	♏ 27	Orion south 8.50.	14	6 59	5 1

MOON'S PHASES.

New Moon, 7d. 12h. 3m., Aft'n. Full Moon, 21d. 12h. 36m., Aft'n.
First Quarter, 14d. 4h. 17m. Ev'g. Last Quarter, 29d. 7h. 29m., Morn.

2d Month. FEBRUARY, 1875. 28 Days.

D. M.	D. W.	Moon South.	Moon Rises or Sets.	Moon's Place. S.	D.	Aspect of Planets and other Miscellanies.	Sun Slow.	Sun Rises.	Sun Sets.
		H. M.	H. M.	S.	D.		M.	H. M.	H. M.
1	M.	9 10	2 40	♐	11	♀ gr. Hel. Lat. N.	14	6 57	5 3
2	Tu.	9 40	3 59	♐	25	☍ ♅ ☉. ☌ ☽ ♀.	14	6 56	5 4
3	W.	10 22	4 54	♑	9	♃ ris. 11.10. [♀ ris. 3.57.	14	6 55	5 5
4	Th.	11 4	5 49	♑	23	Sirius south 9.27.	14	6 54	5 6
5	Fr.	*Spener d.* 1705.		♒	8	☌ ♄ ☉ Orion so. 8.32	14	6 53	5 7
6	Sa.	12 16	☽ sets.	♒	23	6th. ☌ ☽ ♄. 7° s. 6.24	14	6 51	5 9

(6) **Quinquag'a Sun.] Luke 18. 31-43. I. Cor. 13. 1-13. [Day's l., 10h. 20m.**

7	**S.**	1 12	6 58	♓	8	☌ ☽ ☿. ♂ rises 11.54.	14	6 50	5 10
8	M.	2 8	8 10	♓	23	Arcturus rises 7.36.	15	6 49	5 11
9	Tu.	*Shrove Tuesd'y.*		♈	8	☿ in ☊. Antares ris. 3.25	15	6 48	5 12
10	W.	*Ash Wednesday*		♈	22	☽ in per. ☊. ♃ ris. 10.58.	15	6 47	5 13
11	Th.	4 36	11 51	♉	7	♀ rises 3.55.	15	6 46	5 14
12	Fr.	5 30	morn.	♉	21	☿ sets 6.12.	15	6 45	5 15
13	Sa.	6 25	12 49	♊	5	13th. ☿ gr. elong. E.	15	6 44	5 16

(7) **1st Sun. in Lent.] Matt. 4. 1-11. II. Cor. 6. 1-10. [Day's l., 10h. 36m.**

14	**S.**	7 27	1 54	♊	19	☿ in Perihelion.	14	6 42	5 18
15	M.	8 30	3 6	♋	3	♃ stationary.	14	6 41	5 19
16		*Melanchthon b.* 1497		♋	17	♂ rises 11.41.	14	6 40	5 20
17	W.	*Ember Day.*		♌	0	♀ gr. elong. West.	14	6 39	5 21
18	Th.	*Luther d.* 1546.		♌	14	☿ stationary. ☉ enters ♓.	14	6 37	5 23
19	Fr.	11 38	6 31	♌	28	♀ rises 3.56. [9.12.	14	6 36	5 24
20	Sa.	morn.	☽ rises	♍	12	20th. Procyon south	14	6 35	5 25

(8) **2d Sun. in Lent.] Matt. 15. 21-28. I. Thes. 4. 1-7. [Day's l., 10h. 52m.**

21	**S.**	12 21	6 29	♍	26	Pollux south 9.36.	14	6 34	5 26
22		*Washington b.* 1732		♎	8	Spica rises 9.28.	14	6 33	5 27
23	Tu.	2 20	8 26	♎	22	☋. Regulus rises 11.22.	14	6 32	5 28
24	W.	3 10	9 29	♏	6	☿ gr. Hel. Lat. N.	14	6 31	5 29
25	Th.	3 59	10 40	♏	18	☌ ☽ ♃. ♃ rises 10.25.	13	6 29	5 31
26	Fr.	4 42	11 55	♏	29	☽ in apo. □ ♂ ☉.	13	6 28	5 32
27	Sa.	5 38	morn.	♐	10	♂ rises 11 30.	13	6 27	5 33

(9) **3d Sun. in Lent.] Luke 11. 14-28. Ephes. 5. 1-13. [Day's l., 11h. 8m.**

28	**S.**	6 39	12 31	♐	22	28th. ♀ rises 3.59. [☌ ☽ ♂.	13	6 26	5 34

MOON'S PHASES.

New Moon, 6d. 2h. 49m., Morn. Full Moon, 20d. 2h. 56m., Morn.
First Quar., 13d. 12h. 15m., Morn. Last Quart., 28d. 4h. 46m., Morn.

Venus (♀) is Morning Star till the 23d of September; then Evening Star till the end of the year.

Saturn (♄) is in conjunct'n with the Sun 5th this mo. and cannot be seen.

3d Month. MARCH, 1875. 31 Days.

D. M.	D. W.	Moon South.	Moon Rises or Sets.	Moon's Place.		Aspect of Planets and other Miscellanies.	Sun Slow.	Sun Rises.	Sun Sets.
		H. M.	H. M.	S.	D.		M.	H. M.	H. M.
1	M.	7 33	1 34	♑	4	☌☿☉ Inferior.	13	6 24	5 36
2	Tu.	8 28	2 38	♑	16	♃ rises 10.5.	12	6 23	5 37
3	W.	9 24	3 40	♑	29	☌☽♀. ♀ rises 4.4.	12	6 22	5 38
4	Th.	10 4	4 32	♒	14	Sirius south 7.37.	12	6 20	5 40
5	Fr.	10 44	5 12	♒	29	☌☽♄. ♄ rises 5.19.	12	6 19	5 41
6	Sa.	11 20	5 50	♓	14	☌☽☿. Reg. south 10.54.	11	6 18	5 42

(10) 4th Sun. in Lent.] John 6. 1-15. Gal. 4. 21-31. [Day's l., 11h. 26m.

7	**S.**	11 56	☽ sets.	♓	29	7th. ♂ rises 11.24.	11	6 17	5 43
8	M.	12 46	6 58	♈	15	☊. ♃ rises 9.41.	11	6 15	5 45
9	Tu.	1 36	7 59	♈	29	Rigel sets 11.20.	11	6 14	5 46
10	W.	2 25	8 40	♉	15	☽ in per. ♀ rises 4.6.	10	6 12	5 48
11	Th.	3 19	9 30	♉	29	♄ rises 5.0.	10	6 11	5 49
12	Fr.	4 15	10 21	♊	13	Wega rises 10 24.	10	6 10	5 50
13	Sa.	5 14	11 10	♊	26	Spica rises 8.16.	10	6 9	5 51

(11) 5th Sun. in Lent.] John 8. 46-59. Heb. 9. 11-15. [Day's l., 11h. 44m.

14	**S.**	6 15	morn.	♋	9	14th. ☿ stationary.	9	6 8	5 52
15	M.	7 16	12 4	♋	21	♃ rises 9.18.	9	6 6	5 54
16	Tu.	8 16	1 10	♌	3	Orion sets 12.26.	9	6 5	5 55
17	W.	9 11	2 14	♌	15	Aldebaran sets 11 38.	9	6 4	5 56
18	Th.	10 1	3 18	♌	27	♄ rises 4.51.	8	6 2	5 58
19	Fr.	10 47	4 26	♍	9	♂ rises 11.16.	8	6 1	5 59
20	Sa.	11 30	5 38	♍	21	☉ en ♈. Day and night eq.	8	6 0	6 0

(12) Palm Sun.] Matt. 21. 1-9. Ph. 2. 5-11. I. Cor. 11. 23-32. [Day's l. 12h. 4m.

21	**S.**	morn.	☽ rises.	♎	3	21st. Spring com.	7	5 58	6 2
22	M.	12 50	7 6	♎	14	☋. Rigel sets 10.34.	7	5 57	6 3
23	Tu.	*Francke b. 1660*		♎	26	Regulus south 9.49.	7	5 56	6 4
24	W.	2 22	9 14	♏	8	☌☽♃. ♃ rises 8.48.	6	5 55	6 5
25	Th.	*Maund. Thurs*		♏	21	Sirius south 6.26.	6	5 54	6 6
26	Fr.	*Good Friday.*		♐	1	♄ rises 4.29.	6	5 53	6 7
27	Sa.	4 32	11 24	♐	15	☽ in apo. ♀ rises 4.5.	5	5 51	6 9

(13) Easter Sunday.] Mark 16. 1-8. I. Cor. 5. 6-8. [Day's l., 12h. 22m.

28	**S.**	*Easter Sunday.*		♐	28	☌☽♂. ♂ rises 11.2.	5	5 49	6 11
29	M.	*Easter Mond'y.*		♑	11	29th. ☿ gr. elong. W.	5	5 48	6 12
30	Tu.	7 9	morn.	♑	25	☿ in Aphelion.	4	5 47	6 13
31	W.	8 2	1 36	♒	9	☿ rises 4.59.	4	5 46	6 14

MOON'S PHASES.

New Moon, 7d. 3h. 15m., Aft'n. Full Moon, 21d. 6h. 46m., Eve'g.

First Quar., 14d. 8h. 0m., Morn. Last Quar., 29d. 11h. 19m., Eve'g.

4th Month. APRIL, 1875. 30 Days.

D. M.	D. W.	Moon South.	Moon Rises or Sets.	Moon' Place.		Aspect of Planets and other Miscellanies.	Sun Slow.	Sun Rises.	Sun Sets.
		H. M.	H. M.	S.	D.		M.	H. M.	H. M.
1	Th.	8 42	2 39	♒	23	♃ rises 8.21.	4	5 45	6 15
2	Fr.	9 31	3 49	♓	8	☽☌♄.♀. ♀ rises 4.3.	4	5 43	6 17
3	Sa.	10 10	4 20	♓	23	♄ rises 3.53.	3	5 42	6 18
(14) 1st Sun. aft. Easter.] John 20. 19-31. I. John 5. 4-10. [Day's l., 12h. 40m.									
4	**S.**	10 50	4 46	♈	8	☌☽☿. ♂ rises 10.56.	3	5 40	6 20
5	M.	11 31	5 12	♈	23	☊. Sirius sets 10.42.	3	5 39	6 21
6	Tu.	12 21	☽ sets.	♉	8	6th. ♂ in ☋. [8.24.	2	5 38	6 22
7	W.	1 8	8 34	♉	23	☽ in per. Reg. south	2	5 37	6 23
8	Th.	2 5	9 26	♊	7	♃ rises 7.59.	2	5 36	6 24
9	Fr.	3 6	10 22	♊	21	♄ rises 3.42.	2	5 35	6 25
10	Sa.	4 8	11 18	♋	5	♀ rises 3 59.	1	5 34	6 26
(15) 2d Sun. aft. Easter.] John 10. 11-16. I. Pet. 2. 21-25. [Day's l., 12h. 54m.									
11	**S.**	5 11	morn	♋	18	7* sets 9.50.	1	5 33	6 27
12	M.	6 12	12 12	♌	0	12. Rigel sets 10.22	1	5 32	6 28
13	Tu.	7 7	12 56	♌	12	Wega rises 8.19.	1	5 30	6 30
14	W.	7 59	1 38	♌	24	Orion sets 10.44.	0	5 29	6 31
15	Th.	8 45	2 11	♍	6	♃ south 12.6.	sun	5 28	6 32
16	Fr.	9 29	2 37	♍	18	♄ rises 3.30.	fast	5 26	6 34
17	Sa.	10 10	3 19	♎	0	☍♃☉. ♂ rises 10.42.	0	5 25	6 35
(16) 3d Sun. aft. Easter.] John 16. 16-23. I. Pet. 2. 11-20. [Day's l., 13h. 12m.									
18	*Luth. at Worms* 1521			♎	12	♅ stationary.	1	5 24	6 36
19	*Melanch. d.* 1560.			♎	24	☿ gr. Hel. Lat. S. ☋.	1	5 23	6 37
20	Tu.	morn.	☽ rises.	♏	6	20th. ☌☽♃. ☌ Nep-	1	5 22	6 38
21	W.	12 50	8 16	♏	18	☉ ent. ♉. [tune ☉.	1	5 20	6 40
22	Th.	1 39	9 20	♐	0	☽ in apo. ♀ rises 3.50.	2	5 19	6 41
23	Fr.	2 26	10 10	♐	12	♃ south 11.40.	2	5 18	6 42
24	Sa.	3 17	10 39	♐	25	7* sets 9.10.	2	5 17	6 43
(17) 4th Sun. aft. Easter.] John 16. 5-15. James 1. 16-21. [Day's l., 13h. 28m.									
25	**S.**	*Protest*, 1529.		♑	8	☌☽♂. ♂ rises 10.31.	2	5 16	6 44
26	M.	5 3	morn.	♑	21	Orion sets 10.1.	2	5 15	6 45
27	Tu.	5 55	12 18	♒	5	Sirius sets 9.20.	2	5 13	6 47
28	W.	6 44	1 15	♒	19	28th. ♀ rises 3.44.	3	5 12	6 48
29	Th.	7 34	2 11	♓	3	☌☽♄. ♄ rises 2.50	3	5 11	6 49
30	Fr.	8 22	3 0	♓	18	Antares rises 9.27.	3	5 10	6 50

MOON'S PHASES.

New Moon, 6d. 1h. 30m., Morn. Full Moon, 20d. 11h. 25m., Foren.

First Quar., 12d. 4h. 28m., Aft'n. Last Quar., 28d. 2h. 12m., After'n.

Jupiter (♃) is in opposition with the Sun 17th this mo. and shines all night.

5th Month. MAY, 1875. 31 Days.

D. M.	D. W.	Moon South.	Moon Rises or Sets.	Moon's Place.	Aspect of Planets and other Miscellanies.	Sun Fast.	Sun Rises.	Sun Sets.
		H. M.	H. M.	S. D.		M.	H. M.	H. M.
1	Sa.	9 10	3 26	♈ 1	□♅☉. ♃ so. 11.10.	3	5 9	6 51
(18) 5th Sun. aft. Eas'r.] John 16. 23-30. James 1. 22-27. [Day's l., 13h. 44m.								
2	S.	9 59	3 48	♈ 16	☊. ♀ in Aphel. ☌☽♀.	3	5 8	6 52
3	M.	10 40	4 12	♉ 2	♀ rises 3.55.	3	5 7	6 53
4	Tu.	11 19	4 38	♉ 17	♂ rises 10.23.	3	5 6	6 54
5	W.	12 5	☽ sets.	♊ 1	5th. ☽ in per. ☌☽☿	3	5 5	6 55
6	Th.	*Ascens. Day.*		♊ 15	♄ rises 2.31.	4	5 4	6 56
7	Fr.	1 49	9 43	♊ 29	Spica south 10.21.	4	5 3	6 57
8	*Am. Bib. Soc. f.* 1816			♋ 13	♃ south 10.36.	4	5 2	6 58
(19) Sun. aft. Ascen.] John 15. 26; 16. 4. I. Pet. 4. 7-11. [Day's l., 13h. 58m.								
9	S.	3 58	11 10	♋ 26	☌☿☉ Superior.	4	5 1	6 59
10	M.	4 59	11 52	♌ 8	♀ rises 3.32.	4	5 0	7 0
11	*Am. Tr. Soc. f.* 1825			♌ 20	♂ rises 10.11.	4	4 59	7 1
12	W.	6 41	12 31	♍ 2	12th. Libræ S. 11.44.	4	4 58	7 2
13	Th.	7 27	1 10	♍ 14	☿ in Perihelion.	4	4 57	7 3
14	Fr.	8 10	1 40	♍ 26	♄ rises 1.59.	4	4 56	7 4
15	Sa.	8 52	2 11	♎ 8	☋. 7* sets 7.38.	4	4 55	7 5
(20) Whit Sun., or Pen'cot.] John 14. 23-31. Acts 2. 1-12. [Day's l., 14h. 12m.								
16	S.	*Whit Sunday.*		♎ 20	□♄☉. ♂ rises 9.50.	4	4 54	7 6
17	M.	*Whit Monday.*		♏ 2	☌☽♃. ♃ south 9.56.	4	4 53	7 7
18	Tu.	10 50	3 30	♏ 14	♂ stationary.	4	4 52	7 8
19	W.	*Ember Day.*		♏ 26	♀ rises 3.25.	4	4 51	7 9
20	Th.	morn.	☽ rises.	♐ 9	20th. ☽ in apo.	4	4 50	7 10
21	Fr.	12 24	8 56	♐ 22	☉ enters ♊.	4	4 50	7 10
22	Sa.	1 14	9 38	♑ 5	♄ rises 1.12.	3	4 49	7 11
(21) Trinity Sunday.] John 3. 1-15. Rom. 11. 33-36. [Day's l., 14h. 24m.								
23	S.	2 6	10 34	♑ 18	☌☽♂. ☿ gr. Hel. Lat. N.	3	4 48	7 12
24	M.	2 58	11 10	♒ 2	♂ rises 9.30.	3	4 48	7 12
25	Tu.	3 49	11 51	♒ 16	♀ gr. Hel. Lat. S.	3	4 47	7 13
26	W.	*Calvin d.* 1564.		♓ 0	Regulus sets 12 31.	3	4 47	7 13
27	Th.	*Corpus Christi.*		♓ 14	☌☽♄. ♄ rises 12.49.	3	4 46	7 14
28	Fr.	6 26	1 24	♓ 28	28th. ♀ rises 3.16	3	4 46	7 14
29	Sa.	7 30	2 11	♈ 12	☊. ♃ south 9.16.	3	4 45	7 15
(22) 1st Sun. aft. Trin.] Luke 16. 19-31. I. John 4. 16-21. [Day's l., 14h. 30m.								
30	S.	8 36	2 37	♈ 26	Spica south 8.48.	3	4 45	7 15
31	M.	9 31	3 2	♉ 11	Pollux sets 10.53.	3	4 44	7 16

MOON'S PHASES.

New Moon, 5d. 10h. 0m., Fore'n. Full Moon, 20d. 3h. 45m., Morn.

First Quar., 12d. 2h. 31m., Morn. Last Quar., 28d. 1h. 25m., Morn.

6th Month. JUNE, 1875. 30 Days.

D. M.	D. W.	Moon South.	Moon Rises or Sets.	Moon's Place.		Aspect of Planets and other Miscellanies.	Sun Fast.	Sun Rises.	Sun Sets.
		H M.	H. M.	S.	D.		M.	H. M.	H. M.
1	Tu.	10 26	3 26	♉	25	☌☽♀. ♀ rises 3.14.	3	4 43	7 17
2	W.	11 17	3 52	♊	9	Libræ south 10.3.	2	4 43	7 17
3	Th.	11 56	☽sets.	♊	23	3d. ☽ in per.	2	4 43	7 17
4	Fr.	12 50	8 50	♋	7	♃ south 8.56.	2	4 42	7 18
5	Sa.	1 40	9 32	♋	20	☌☽☿. ♄ rises 12.28.	2	4 42	7 18

(23) 2d Sun. aft. Trin.] Luke 14. 16-24. I. John 3. 13-18. [Day's l., 14h. 36m.

D. M.	D. W.	Moon South.	Moon Rises or Sets.	Moon's Place.		Aspect of Planets and other Miscellanies.	Sun Fast.	Sun Rises.	Sun Sets.
6	S.	2 44	10 10	♌	3	♄ stationary.	2	4 42	7 18
7	M	3 43	10 40	♌	16	♂ rises 8.50.	1	4 41	7 19
8	Tu.	4 36	11 28	♌	28	♀ rises 3.8.	1	4 41	7 19
9	W.	5 24	morn.	♍	10	☿ gr. elong. East.	1	4 41	7 19
10	Th.	6 8	12 14	♍	22	10th. ☿ sets 8.13.	1	4 40	7 20
11	Fr.	6 47	12 39	♎	4	♄ rises 12 4.	0	4 40	7 20
12	Sa.	7 28	1 5	♎	16	☋. Altair south 12.22.	0	4 40	7 20

(24) 3d Sun. aft. Trin.] Luke 15. 1-10. I. Pet. 5. 6-11. [Day's l., 14h. 40m.

D. M.	D. W.	Moon South.	Moon Rises or Sets.	Moon's Place.		Aspect of Planets and other Miscellanies.	Sun Fast.	Sun Rises.	Sun Sets.
13	S.	8 8	1 29	♎	28	☌☽♃. ♃ south 8 0.	sun	4 40	7 20
14	M.	8 48	1 55	♏	10	♂ rises 8.1.	slo.	4 39	7 21
15	Tu.	9 34	2 19	♏	22	☽ in apo. ☿ in ☋.	0	4 39	7 21
16	W.	10 18	2 44	♐	5	♄ rises 11.44.	0	4 39	7 21
17	Th.	11 8	3 20	♐	18	♀ rises 3.2.	1	4 39	7 21
18	Fr.	morn.	☽rises.	♑	1	18th. ☌☽♂.	1	4 39	7 21
19	Sa.	12 50	9 0	♑	14	♃ stationary.	1	4 39	7 21

(25) 4th Sun. aft. Trin.] Luke 6. 36-42. Rom. 8. 18-23. [Day's l., 14h. 42m.

D. M.	D. W.	Moon South.	Moon Rises or Sets.	Moon's Place.		Aspect of Planets and other Miscellanies.	Sun Fast.	Sun Rises.	Sun Sets.
20	S.	1 44	9 40	♑	28	☍♂☉. ♂ south 11.56.	1	4 39	7 21
21	M.	2 36	10 13	♒	12	☉ ent. ♋. longest day.	1	4 38	7 22
22	Tu.	3 25	11 0	♒	26	Summer commences.	2	4 39	7 21
23	W.	4 12	11 26	♓	10	☿ stationary. ☌☽♄.	2	4 39	7 21
24	Th.	4 58	11 54	♓	25	♄ rises 11.16.	2	4 39	7 21
25	*Augsb. Conf.* 1530.			♈	9	☊. ♃ sets 12.40.	2	4 39	7 21
26	Sa.	6 28	12 12	♈	23	26th. ☿ in Aphelion.	3	4 39	7 21

(26) 5th Sun. aft. Trin.] Luke 5. 1-11. I. Pet. 3. 8-15. [Day's l., 14h. 42m.

D. M.	D. W.	Moon South.	Moon Rises or Sets.	Moon's Place.		Aspect of Planets and other Miscellanies.	Sun Fast.	Sun Rises.	Sun Sets.
27	S.	7 18	12 36	♉	7	♀ rises 2.59.	3	4 39	7 21
28	M.	8 12	1 4	♉	21	♂ south 11.21.	3	4 39	7 21
29	Tu.	9 9	1 38	♊	5	Antares south 9.47.	3	4 40	7 20
30	W.	10 12	2 20	♊	19	Spica sets 9.8.	3	4 40	7 20

MOON'S PHASES.

New Moon, 3d. 5h. 15m., Aft'n. **Full Moon, 18d. 6h. 51m., Eve'g.**
First Quar., 10d. 2h. 50m., Aft'n. **Last Quar., 26d. 9h. 34m., Morn.**

Mars (♂) is in opposition with the Sun 20th this mo. and shines all night.

7th Month. JULY, 1875. 31 Days.

D. M.	D. W.	Moon South.	Moon Rises or Sets.	Moon's Place.		Aspect of Planets and other Miscellanies.	Sun Slow.	Sun Rises.	Sun Sets.
		H. M.	H. M.	S.	D.		M.	H. M.	H. M.
1	Th.	10 54	2 46	♋	2	☽ in per. ☌ ☽ ♀. ♀ r. 3.0.	3	4 40	7 20
2	Fr.	11 38	3 20	♋	15	♄ rises 10.42.	4	4 40	7 20
3	Sa.	12 20	☽ sets.	♋	29	3d. ☉ in apo. ☌ ☽ ☿	4	4 41	7 19
(27) 6th Sun. aft. Trin.] Matt. 5. 20-26. Rom. 6. 3-11. [Day's l., 14h. 38m.									
4	*Independence,*	1776		♌	12	Dog Days begin.	4	4 41	7 19
5	M.	2 22	9 45	♌	25	♂ south 10.50.	4	4 41	7 19
6	Tu.	3 16	10 12	♍	7	☌ ☿ ☉ inferior.	4	4 42	7 18
7	W.	4 0	10 36	♍	19	♃ sets 11.57.	4	4 42	7 18
8	Th.	4 44	10 54	♎	1	Wega south 11.19.	5	4 42	7 18
9	Fr.	5 26	11 20	♎	13	☋. ♄ rises 10.10.	5	4 43	7 17
10	Sa.	6 6	11 48	♎	24	10th. ☌ ☽ ♃.	5	4 43	7 17
(28) 7th Sun. aft. Trin.] Mark 8. 1-9. Rom. 6. 19-23. [Day's l., 14h. 34m.									
11	**S.**	6 47	morn.	♏	6	7° rises 12.48.	5	4 43	7 17
12	M.	7 30	22 38	♏	18	Antares south 8.51.	5	4 44	7 16
13	Tu.	8 15	1 8	♐	0	☽ in apo. ♀ rises 3.10.	5	4 44	7 16
14	W.	9 4	1 38	♐	13	♂ south 10.24.	5	4 45	7 15
15	Th.	9 55	2 6	♐	26	□ ♃ ☉. ☌ ☽ ♂.	6	4 46	7 14
16	*Melanch. b.*	1497.		♑	10	☿ gr. Hel. Lat. S.	6	4 46	7 14
17	Sa.	11 40	3 4	♑	24	☿ stationary.	6	4 47	7 13
(29) 8th Sun. aft. Trin.] Matt. 7. 15-23. Rom. 8. 12-17. [Day's l., 14h. 26m.									
18	**S.**	morn.	☽ rises.	♒	8	18th. ♃ sets 11.10.	6	4 47	7 13
19	M.	12 22	8 42	♒	22	♄ rises 9.28.	6	4 48	7 12
20	Tu.	1 36	9 8	♓	6	☌ ☿ ♀. ☌ ☽ ♄. ♀ in ☊.	6	4 49	7 11
21	W.	2 58	9 33	♓	21	♀ rises 3.18.	6	4 50	7 10
22	*Dr. Jacobs d.*	1871.		♈	6	☉ enters ♌.	6	4 50	7 10
23	Fr.	4 29	10 25	♈	20	☊. ♂ south 10.4.	6	4 51	7 9
24	Sa.	5 15	10 51	♉	4	♃ sets 10.52.	6	4 52	7 8
(30) 9th Sun. aft. Trin.] Luke 16. 1-9. I. Cor. 10. 6-13. [Day's l., 14h. 14m.									
25	**S.**	6 5	11 18	♉	18	25th. ♂ stationary	6	4 53	7 7
26	*Dr. Schmuck d.*	1873		♊	2	□ Neptune ☉.	6	4 54	7 6
27	Tu.	7 50	morn.	♊	15	☿ gr. elong. West.	6	4 55	7 5
28	W.	8 41	12 26	♊	18	☿ rises 3.57.	6	4 56	7 4
29	Th.	9 32	1 14	♋	12	☽ in per. ♄ rises 8 56.	6	4 57	7 3
30	Fr.	10 21	2 27	♋	25	☌ ☽ ☿. ♂ south 9.39.	6	4 58	7 2
31	Sa.	11 19	3 36	♌	8	☌ ☽ ♀. ♀ rises 3.30.	6	4 59	7 1

MOON'S PHASES.

New Moon, 3d. 12h. 19m., Morn. **Full Moon, 18d. 8h. 21m., Morn.**

First Quar., 10d. 5h. 35m., " **Last Quar., 25d. 3h. 34m., After'n.**

8th Month. AUGUST, 1875. 31 Days.

D. M.	D. W.	Moon South.	Moon Rises or Sets.	Moon's Place.		Aspect of Planets and other Miscellanies.	Sun Slow.	Sun Rises.	Sun Sets.
(31) 10th Sun. aft. Trin.] Luke 19. 41-48. I. Cor. 12. 1-11. [Day's l., 14h. 0m.									
		H. M.	H. M.	S.	D.		M.	H. M.	H. M.
1	**S.**	12 10	☽sets.	♌	20	1st. ♂ so. 9.30.	6	5 0	7 0
2	M.	1 2	7 50	♍	2	Antares so. 7.31.	6	5 1	6 59
3	Tu.	1 48	8 16	♍	14	Altair south 10.52.	6	5 2	6 58
4	W.	2 36	8 41	♍	26	☿ in ☊. Sirius ris. 4.38.	6	5 4	6 56
5	Th.	3 18	9 0	♎	8	☋. ♀ rises 3.51.	6	5 5	6 55
6	Fr.	3 59	9 24	♎	20	Neptune stationary.	6	5 6	6 54
7	Sa.	4 42	9 48	♏	2	☌☽♃. ♃ sets 10.9.	5	5 7	6 53
(32) 11th Sun. aft. Trin.] Luke 18. 9-14. I. Cor. 15. 1-10. [Day's l., 13h. 44m.									
8	**S.**	5 44	10 8	♏	14	8th. ☌ ♅ ☉.	5	5 8	6 52
9	M.	6 21	10 36	♏	26	☿ in Perihelion.	5	5 9	6 51
10	Tu.	6 59	11 26	♐	8	☽ in apo. ☌ ☿ ♀.	5	5 10	6 50
11	W.	7 46	morn.	♐	21	♂ south 8.56.	5	5 11	6 49
12	Th.	8 39	12 16	♑	4	☌☽♂. Dog days end.	5	5 12	6 48
13	Fr.	9 32	1 28	♑	18	Orion rises 1.46.	5	5 13	6 47
14	Sa.	10 26	2 42	♒	2	♀ rises 4.12.	4	5 14	6 46
(33) 12th Sun. aft. Trin.] Mark 7. 31-37. II. Cor. 3. 4-11. [Day's l., 13h. 30m.									
15	**S.**	11 16	3 59	♒	17	☍ ♄ ☉. ♄ south 12.6.	4	5 15	6 45
16	M.	morn.	☽rises.	♓	1	16th. ☌ ☽ ♄.	4	5 16	6 44
17	Tu.	12 4	7 38	♓	16	♃ sets 9.28.	4	5 17	6 43
18	W.	12 52	8 3	♈	1	7* rises 10.21.	4	5 18	6 42
19	Th.	1 42	8 29	♈	16	☊. ☿ gr. Hel. Lat. N.	3	5 19	6 41
20	Fr.	2 54	9 0	♉	0	♂ south 8.25.	3	5 20	6 40
21	Sa.	3 59	9 34	♉	14	Sirius rises 3.32.	3	5 22	6 38
(34) 13th Sun. aft. Trin.] Luke 10. 23-37. Gal. 3. 15-22. [Day's l., 13h. 14m.									
22	**S.**	5 6	10 20	♉	28	☌ ☿ ☉ sup. ☉ ent. ♍.	3	5 23	6 37
23	M.	6 16	11 4	♊	12	23d. ♀ in Perihelion.	2	5 24	6 36
24	Tu	6 58	morn.	♊	25	☽ in per.	2	5 26	6 34
25	W.	7 54	12 2	♋	9	♄ south 11.30.	2	5 27	6 33
26	Th.	8 55	1 4	♋	22	♃ sets 9.9.	2	5 28	6 32
27	Fr.	9 50	2 10	♌	4	Altair south 9.18.	1	5 29	6 31
28	Sa.	10 30	3 26	♌	17	Orion rises 12.48.	1	5 30	6 30
(35) 14th Sun. aft. Trin.] Luke 17. 11-19. Gal. 5. 16-24. [Day's l., 12h. 58m.									
29	**S.**	*St. John beh.*		♌	29	♂ south 8.1.	1	5 31	6 29
30	M.	11 50	☽sets.	♍	11	30th. ☌☽♀.	0	5 32	6 28
31	Tu.	12 44	7 2	♍	23	☌☽☿. Spica sets 8. 2.	0	5 33	6 27

MOON'S PHASES.

New Moon, 1d. 8h. 22m., Morn. **Full Moon, 16d. 8h. 28m., Eve'g.**
First Quar., 8d. 10h. 25m., Eve'g. **Last Quar., 23d. 8h. 33m., Eve'g.**
New Moon, 30d. 6h. 36m., Even'g.

Saturn (♄) is in opposition with the Sun 15th this mo. and shines all night.

9th Month. SEPTEMBER, 1875. 30 Days.

D. M.	D. W.	Moon South.	Moon Rises or Sets.	Moon's Place. S.	D.	Aspect of Planets and other Miscellanies.	Sun Fast.	Sun Rises.	Sun Sets.
		H. M.	H. M.				M.	H. M.	H. M.
1	W.	1 28	7 30	♎	5	Sirius rises 2.49.	0	5 34	6 26
2	Th.	2 14	7 54	♎	17	☋. ♂ south 7.56.	0	5 35	6 25
3	Fr.	2 51	8 18	♎	29	♄ south 10.42.	1	5 36	6 24
4	Sa.	3 34	8 42	♏	11	☌ ☽ ♃. ♃ sets 8.29.	1	5 37	6 23

(36) 15th Sun. aft. Trin.] Matt. 6. 24-34. Gal. 5. 25. 6-10. [Day's l., 12h. 42m.

D. M.	D. W.	Moon South.	Moon Rises or Sets.	Moon's Place. S.	D.	Aspect of Planets and other Miscellanies.	Sun Fast.	Sun Rises.	Sun Sets.
5	**S.**	4 16	9 10	♏	23	Orion rises 2.45.	1	5 39	6 21
6	*Dr. Muhlenb. b.* 1711			♐	5	☽ in apogee.	2	5 40	6 20
7	Tu	5 39	10 26	♐	16	7th. Spica sets 7.48.	2	5 41	6 19
8	W.	6 27	11 22	♐	29	Antares sets 9.37	2	5 42	6 18
9	Th	7 22	morn.	♑	12	☌ ☽ ♂. ♂ sets 12.0.	3	5 44	6 16
10	Fr.	8 15	12 26	♑	26	♂ gr. Hel. Lat. S.	3	5 45	6 15
11	Sa.	9 8	1 38	♒	10	7° rises 8.46.	3	5 46	6 14

(37) 16th Sun. aft. Trin.] Luke 7. 11-17. Ephes. 3. 13-21. [Day's l., 12h. 26m.

D. M.	D. W.	Moon South.	Moon Rises or Sets.	Moon's Place. S.	D.	Aspect of Planets and other Miscellanies.	Sun Fast.	Sun Rises.	Sun Sets.
12	**S.**	9 58	2 56	♒	24	☌ ☽ ♄. ♄ south 9.59.	4	5 47	6 13
13	M.	10 44	3 40	♓	9	♃ sets 8.0.	4	5 48	6 12
14	Tu	11 36	4 39	♓	24	♀ gr. Hel. Lat. N.	5	5 50	6 10
15	*Ember Day*		6 59	♈	9	15. ☊. Pol. r. 12.18.	5	5 51	6 9
16	Th.	morn.	☽ rises.	♈	25	Rigel rises 11.43.	5	5 53	6 7
17	Fr.	1 40	7 42	♉	10	Antares sets 9.12.	6	5 54	6 6
18	Sa.	2 49	8 30	♉	24	☽ in per. ♂ sets 11.42.	6	5 55	6 5

(38) 17th Sun. aft. Trin.] Luke 14. 1-11. Ephes. 4. 1-6. [Day's l., 12h. 8m.

D. M.	D. W.	Moon South.	Moon Rises or Sets.	Moon's Place. S.	D.	Aspect of Planets and other Miscellanies.	Sun Fast.	Sun Rises.	Sun Sets.
19	**S.**	3 46	9 18	♊	8	Arcturus sets 9.31.	6	5 56	6 4
20	M.	4 47	10 12	♊	22	♃ sets 7.39.	7	5 57	6 3
21	Tu.	5 48	11 6	♋	5	♄ south 9.28.	7	5 58	6 2
22	W.	6 51	morn.	♋	19	22d. ☿ in Aphelion.	7	5 59	6 1
23	Th.	7 50	12 8	♌	1	☌ ♀ ☉ sup. ☉ enters ♎.	8	6 0	6 0
24	Fr.	8 44	1 14	♌	14	Aut'mn com [Day & night	8	6 1	5 59
25	Sa.	9 37	2 16	♌	26	Sirius r. 1.28. [equal.	8	6 2	5 58

(39) 18th Sun. aft. Trin.] Matt. 22. 34-46. I. Cor. 1. 4-9. [Day's l., 11h. 52m.

D. M.	D. W.	Moon South.	Moon Rises or Sets.	Moon's Place. S.	D.	Aspect of Planets and other Miscellanies.	Sun Fast.	Sun Rises.	Sun Sets.
26	**S.**	10 8	3 10	♍	8	♂ sets 11.28.	9	6 4	5 56
27	M.	10 49	4 0	♍	20	Wega south 6.14.	9	6 5	5 55
28	Tu.	11 30	4 41	♎	2	☋ Andromeda so. 11.40.	9	6 7	5 53
29	*Gus. Vasa d.* 1560			♎	14	29th. ☉ eclip. visible	10	6 8	5 52
30	Th.	12 50	6 30	♎	26	♄ south 8.56.	10	6 10	5 50

MOON'S PHASES.

First Quar., 7d. 4h. 32m., Aft'n. Last Quar., 22d. 1h. 55m., Morn'g.

Full Moon, 15d. 7h. 36m., Morn. New Moon, 29d. 7h. 50m., "

Venus (♀) is in superior conjunction above the Sun on the 23d of this month; passes from Morning to Evening Star.

| 10th Month. | OCTOBER, 1875. | 31 Days. |

D. M.	D. W.	Moon South.	Moon Rises or Sets.	Moon' Place.	Aspect of Planets and other Miscellanies.	Sun Fast.	Sun Rises.	Sun Sets.
		H. M.	H. M.	S. D.		M.	H. M.	H. M.
1	Fr.	1 31	6 55	♏ 7	☽♂☿.♃.♃ sets 6.54. ♈	10	6 11	5 49
2	Sa.	2 12	7 20	♏ 19	♄ south 8.50.	11	6 12	5 48

(40) 19th Sun. aft. Trin.] Matt. 9. 1-3. Ephes. 4. 22-28. [Day's l., 11h. 34m.

3	S.	2 54	7 52	♐ 1	Sirius rises 12 58.	11	6 13	5 47
4	M.	3 36	8 31	♐ 13	☽ in apo. ♂ in Perihel'n.	11	6 14	5 46
5	Tu	4 19	9 20	♐ 26	♂☿♃. ☿ sets 6 44. ♅	12	6 16	5 44
6	W.	5 11	10 18	♑ 9	☿ gr. elong. East.	12	6 17	5 43
7	Muhlenb. d. 1787.			♑ 22	☽7.♂☽♂.♂ s. 11.14.	12	6 19	5 41
8	Fr.	6 56	morn.	♒ 5	☽ 7° rises 7.25.	12	6 20	5 40
9	Sa.	7 48	12 32	♒ 19	Rigel rises 9.47.	13	6 21	5 39

(41) 20th Sun. aft. Trin.] Matt. 22. 1-14. Ephes. 5. 15-21. [Day's l., 11h. 16m.

10	S.	8 38	1 52	♓ 3	♂☽♄. ♄ south 8.36.	13	6 22	5 38
11	M.	Zwingli d. 1531		♓ 19	♃ sets 6.14.	13	6 24	5 36
12	Tu	10 20	4 10	♈ 3	☿ gr. Hel. Lat. S. ☊.	13	6 25	5 35
13	W.	11 12	5 1	♈ 18	Arctur. sets 8.10.	13	6 26	5 34
14	Th.	morn.	☽rises.	♉ 3	♋14th. Orion ris. 10.1.	14	6 27	5 33
15	Fr.	12 30	5 57	♉ 18	☽ Fomal south 9:28.	14	6 28	5 32
16	Sa.	1 31	6 32	♊ 3	☽ in per. ♂ sets 11.1.	14	6 29	5 31

(42) 21st Sun. aft. Trin.] John 4. 47-54. Ephes. 6. 10-17. [Day's l., 10h. 58m.

17	S.	2 34	7 16	♊ 17	♃ sets 5.59.	15	6 31	5 29
18	M.	3 38	8 8	♋ 1	☿ stationary. ♎	15	6 32	5 28
19	Tu.	4 34	9 4	♋ 15	Altair south 9.6.	15	6 33	5 27
20	W.	5 16	10 6	♋ 28	Antares sets 7.2.	15	6 34	5 26
21	Th.	5 57	11 12	♌ 11	☾21st. ♄ south 8.6.	15	6 36	5 24
22	Fr.	6 50	morn.	♌ 23	☽ Sirius rises 11.49.	15	6 37	5 23
23	Gen. Syn. org 1820		♍ 5	□♂☉. ☉ enters ♏.	16	6 39	5 21

(43) 22d Sun. aft. Trin.] Matt. 18. 23-35. Phil. 1. 3-11. [Day's l., 10h. 40m.

24	S.	8 20	1 20	♍ 17	♄ stationary.	16	6 40	5 20
25	M.	9 2	2 22	♍ 29	♂♀♃. ♀ Neptune ☉.	16	6 41	5 19
26	Tu	9 46	3 25	♎ 11	♂☿♃. ♘.	16	6 42	5 18
27	W.	10 34	4 23	♎ 23	♂ sets 10.48.	16	6 43	5 17
28	Th.	11 26	5 22	♏ 5	Rigel rises 9.25.	16	6 44	5 16
29	Fr.	12 22	☽sets.	♏ 17	♋29th. ☽♂☿.♃.♀.	16	6 46	5 14
30	Sa.	12 59	5 40	♏ 29	♂☿☉ inferior.	16	6 47	5 13

(44) 23d Sun. aft. Trin.] Matt. 22. 15-22. Phil. 3. 17-21. [Day's l., 10h. 24m.

| 31 | S. | Reform'n, 1517 | ♐ 11 | ♀ Sets 5.35, Even'g Star | 16 | 6 48 | 5 12 |

MOON'S PHASES.

First Quar., 7d. 11h. 0m., Fore'n.   Last Quar., 21d. 9h. 8m., Eve'g.
Full Moon, 14d. 6h. 11m., Eve'g.   New Moon, 29d. 12h. 7m., Morn.

11th Month. NOVEMBER, 1875. 30 Days.

D. M.	D. W.	Moon South.	Moon Rises or Sets.	Moon's Place. S.	D.	Aspect of Planets and other Miscellanies.	Sun Fast.	Sun Rises.	Sun Sets.
		H. M.	H. M.	S.	D.		M.	H. M.	H. M.
1	M.	2 20	7 19	♐	23	☽ in apogee.	16	6 49	5 11
2	Tu.	3 6	8 16	♑	5	Sirius rises 11.6.	16	6 50	5 10
3	W.	3 56	9 20	♑	18	♂ sets 10.40.	16	6 51	5 9
4	Th.	4 40	10 11	♒	1	☌♃☉. ♀ sets 5.34.	16	6 52	5 8
5	Fr.	5 26	10 53	♒	14	☿ in Perihel. ☌☽♂.	16	6 53	5 7
6	Sa.	6 12	11 40	♒	28	6th. ☌☽♄.	16	6 54	5 6
(45) 24th Sun. aft. Trin.] Matt. 9. 18-26. Col. 1. 9-14. [Day's l., 10h. 10m.									
7	**S.**	7 9	morn.	♓	12	☿ stationary.	16	6 55	5 5
8	M.	7 58	12 50	♓	26	7* south 12.44.	16	6 56	5 4
9	Tu.	8 43	2 4	♈	11	♀ in ☋. ☊.	16	6 57	5 3
10	W.	*Luther b.*	1483.	♈	26	Altair sets 11.12.	16	6 58	5 2
11	Th.	10 22	4 12	♉	11	♀ sets 5.33.	16	6 59	5 1
12	Fr.	11 16	5 19	♉	26	□♄☉. ♄ sets 11.41.	16	7 0	5 0
13	Sa.	morn.	☽rises.	♊	11	13th ☽ in per.	15	7 1	4 59
(46) 25th Sun. aft. Trin.] Matt. 24. 15-28. I. Thes. 4. 13-18. [Day's l., 9h. 56m.									
14	**S.**	12 24	5 49	♊	25	♂ sets 10.31.	15	7 2	4 58
15	M.	1 30	6 44	♋	9	☿ gr. elong. West.	15	7 3	4 57
16	Tu.	2 38	7 49	♋	23	☿ rises 6.3.	15	7 4	4 56
17	W.	3 42	8 59	♌	6	Aldebaran rises 6.2.	15	7 5	4 55
18	Th.	4 49	10 1	♌	19	♄ sets 11.23.	15	7 6	4 54
19	Fr.	5 52	11 10	♍	2	19. Sirius ris. 10.0.	14	7 7	4 53
20	Sa.	6 50	morn.	♍	14	♀ sets 5.32.	14	7 8	4 52
47) 26th Sun. aft. Trin.] Matt. 25. 31-46. II Pet. 3. 3-14.] Day's l., 9h., 42m.									
21	**S.**	7 32	12 12	♍	26	☌♂♄. Androm. so. 8 12.	14	7 9	4 51
22	M.	8 18	1 13	♎	8	☋. ☉ enters ♐.	14	7 10	4 50
23	Tu.	9 0	2 19	♎	19	Orion rises 7.22.	13	7 10	4 50
24	W.	9 40	3 30	♏	1	♄ sets 11.4.	13	7 11	4 49
25	Th.	10 22	4 42	♏	13	☌☿♃. ♅ stationary.	13	7 12	4 48
26	Fr.	11 6	5 59	♏	25	☽☌♃. ☿.	12	7 12	4 48
27	Sa.	11 50	☽sets	♐	7	27th. ♂ sets 10.19.	12	7 13	4 47
(48) 1st Sun. in Advent.] Matt. 21. 1-9. Rom. 13. 11-14. [Day's l., 9h. 32m.									
28	**S.**	*Advent*	5 22	♐	19	☽ in apo. ♃ r. 5.49 morn.	12	7 14	4 46
29	M.	1 11	6 20	♑	2	☌☽♀. ♀ sets 5.48.	11	7 14	4 46
30	Tu.	1 52	7 31	♑	15	Arietis south 9.32.	11	7 15	4 45

MOON'S PHASES.

First Quar., 6d. 4h. 47m., Morn. **Last Quar., 19d. 7h. 32m., Eve'g.**

Full Moon, 13d. 4h. 24m., " **New Moon, 27d. 6h. 39m., "**

Jupiter (♃) is in conjunction with the Sun the 4th of this month, and cannot be seen.

12th Month. DECEMBER, 1875. 31 Days.

D. M.	D. W.	Moon South.	Moon Rises or Sets.	Moon's Place.		Aspect of Planets and other Miscellanies.	Sun Fast.	Sun Rises.	Sun Sets.
		H. M.	H. M.	S.	D.		M.	H. M.	H. M.
1	W.	2 43	8 32	♑	28	Sirius rises 9.6.	11	7 15	4 45
2	Th.	3 32	9 21	♒	11	Altair sets 9.32.	10	7 16	4 44
3	Fr.	4 20	10 17	♒	24	♄ sets 10.40.	10	7 16	4 44
4	Sa.	5 4	10 48	♓	8	☽☌♄. ♂. ♂ sets 10 10.	10	7 17	4 43
(49) 2d Sun. in Adv.] Luke 21. 25-36. Rom. 15. 4-13. [Day's l., 9h. 26m.									
5	S.	5 50	11 36	♓	22	5th. ♀ sets 5.58.	9	7 17	4 43
6	M.	6 34	morn.	♈	6	☽ ☊. ♃ rises 5.31.	9	7 18	4 42
7	Tu.	7 29	12 58	♈	20	Regulus rises 10.21.	8	7 18	4 42
8	W.	8 26	2 12	♉	5	Fomal sets 9 56.	8	7 19	4 41
9	Th.	9 24	3 30	♉	20	♄ sets 10.10.	7	7 19	4 41
10	Fr.	10 20	4 39	♊	4	7* south 10.29.	6	7 19	4 41
11	Sa.	11 10	5 41	♊	19	Orion rises 6.8.	6	7 20	4 40
(50) 3d Sun. in Adv.] Matt. 11. 2-10. I. Cor. 4. 1-5. [Day's l., 9h. 20m.									
12	S.	morn.	☽rises.	♋	3	12th. ☽ in per.	6	7 20	4 40
13	M.	12 22	5 26	♋	17	♀ in Aphelion.	5	7 20	4 40
14	*Washington d.*1799			♌	1	♀ sets 6.8.	5	7 20	4 40
15	W.	*Ember Day.*		♌	14	♂ sets 9.58.	5	7 21	4 39
16	Th.	3 40	8 50	♌	27	♃ rises 4 52.	4	7 21	4 39
17	Fr.	4 31	10 10	♍	10	Aldebaran south 10.51.	4	7 21	4 39
18	Sa.	5 25	11 21	♍	22	Arietis south 8.16.	3	7 21	4 39
(51) 4th Sun. in Adv.] John 1. 19-28. Phil. 4. 4-7. [Day's l., 9h. 18m.									
19	S.	6 11	morn.	♎	4	19th. ☿ in Aphelion.	3	7 21	4 39
20	M.	7 8	12 18	♎	16	☋. ♄ sets 9.45.	2	7 21	4 39
21	Tu.	7 52	1 17	♎	28	♀ sets 6.20.	2	7 21	4 39
22	W.	8 32	2 16	♏	10	☉ ent. ♑. Shortest day.	1	7 22	4 38
23	Th.	9 14	3 22	♏	22	Winter commences.	1	7 21	4 39
24	Fr.	9 56	4 29	♐	4	☌☽♃. ♃ rises 4.25.	sun	7 21	4 39
25	Sa.	*Christmas.*		♐	16	☽ in apo ♂ sets 9.46.	slo.	7 21	4 39
(52) Sun. after Christmas.] Luke 2. 33-40. Gal. 4. 1-7. [Day's l., 9h. 18m.									
26	S.	11 18	6 50	♐	28	☌☿☉ superior.	1	7 21	4 39
27	M.	11 58	☽sets.	♑	11	27th ☌☽☿.	1	7 21	4 39
28	Tu.	12 39	5 42	♑	24	Orion south 11.18.	2	7 21	4 39
29	*Dr. B. Kurtz d.*1865			♒	4	☌☽♀. ♀ sets 6.30.	2	7 21	4 39
30	Th.	2 16	8 10	♒	21	Sirius south 12.4.	3	7 20	4 40
31	Fr.	3 4	9 22	♓	5	☌☽♄. ♄ sets 9 12.	3	7 20	4 40

MOON'S PHASES.

First Quar., 5d. 8h. 51m., Even'g. Last Quar., 19d. 9h. 50m., Morn.

Full Moon, 12d. 2h. 40m., After'n. New Moon, 27d. 1h. 59m., Aft'n.

The Standard of Ministerial Education.

A consciousness prevails in our Church that the standard of ministerial education is steadily regaining its level. There never was a time in the history of the Lutheran Church when a high degree of training was decried or undervalued. Nevertheless, it is known that a pressure of circumstances has had the effect, in our own country, to plead for *too many* special cases as exceptions. The spirit of our day is urging men to expedite matters, and to take a "short-cut" toward every position in life; the lax usage of some neighboring denominations has not been without its unhappy effect; to which must be added the earnest cry of congregations for ministers, together with a frequent lack of adequate means for preparation on the part of candidates for the holy office. Such considerations have induced young men in the course of study, as well as the Synods, to yield.

Then look at the result. The expected perfecting in theological culture, *after* entering laborious parishes, has rarely been attained. Men prematurely inducted into the ranks of the Christian ministry have frequently found themselves floundering along through their entire period of pastoral labor, greatly to their own discomfort and chagrin; congregations have seldom realized what they had hoped for; and Synods have had sufficient reason to repent of their leniency.

Blame has been laid upon different agencies, and perhaps not unjustly. But, after all, the great responsibility lies at the door of Synods—the minister-making power. Friends may advise young men, individual ministers may remonstrate, our theological professors may urge and plead; yet if it remains understood that the Synods are willing to smile inordinately upon exceptional cases, then will the Synods themselves hold out a standing temptation to premature applications, and only invite to themselves, from year to year, perplexity and mortification.

Let the proper standard be held in our Synods; not in one or a few only, but in all. Let the case of persons who are worthy exceptions be exceptions indeed. Let there be no hope left that men who cannot stand the test of one Synod, can go elsewhere and slip through the door of another. Then will candidates study with less annoyance from distracting and counteracting influences. They will go on patiently and hopefully, preparing themselves to meet the requisitions of the inspired rule: "Study to show thyself approved unto God, a workman that needeth not to be ashamed, rightly dividing the word of truth." Just such preparation is needed, fully to meet the wants of an age in which popular education is making wonderful advances; to beat down the citadel of every error set up by the cunning of men and the malice of Satan; and to aid, with greater success, in extending the kingdom of our Lord Jesus Christ in the earth.—*S.*

A Prayer to the Crucified Saviour.

We adore Thy perfect love, O merciful Saviour, which humbled Thee even to the cross, that Thou mightest exalt us to the throne of God. Eternally praised be Thy holy name, O blessed Jesus, that for us rebels and outlaws Thou didst vouchsafe to become a curse on the cross, that the great copious stream of divine blessings might flow upon us. Be Thou forever praised who didst condescend to be raised on the cross, as the great antitype of the brazen serpent which was lifted up in the desert, that all who look on Thee in faith may be healed, and live. O fulfill in us all that comforting promise, that after Thy exaltation Thou wouldst draw all men unto Thee! Draw to Thy cross the carnal, the secure, and the unclean; and convince them that, without crucifying their lusts, they can have no share in the blessings which Thou didst procure by Thy crucifixion. Draw to Thy cross the troubled, anxious, and timorous consciences, and heal them by the salutary sight of Thy sufferings. Draw to Thy cross the true disciples, and grant that they may more and more increase in grace and wisdom, and in the knowledge of Thee. O gather together all those who are scattered abroad, far from Thee and the light of Thy gospel, and embrace them with the arms of Thy mercy. Amen.—*Dr. J. Rambach, from Meditations.*

Home Mission Work.

It has an intrinsic merit that, of course, we do not overlook. It has a wider sphere than the gathering together and spiritual culture of those of our own ecclesiastical household. It contemplates all the great ends of the gospel. It is the carrying forward of what Jesus commissioned the disciples to do. Its blessed design is the spread of the gospel, and the salvation of the perishing in our land. May it not be that we have looked upon this work too much in a selfish sectarian light, as having exclusive reference to those who bear our name, who, by reason of change of residence, have gone beyond our boundary? There is a vastly higher design than this: it is the lifting up of the cross before those who are perishing for lack of knowledge; and where this great end is not realized, the work of true evangelization is not being accomplished.—*Rev. M. Rhodes.*

ANOTHER MONUMENT TO LUTHER.—Martin Luther was born in Eisleben, Saxony, November 10th, 1483, and died in the same place, February 18th, 1546. The house in which he was born is still standing, as also the church from which he was buried. An association has been formed in Germany for the purpose of erecting a monument to his memory in the old town, and a letter from Dr. Dorner to Dr. Conrad, of Philadelphia, calls the attention of Lutherans in this country to the effort, and invites their participation in it.

Attend Your Own Church.

Sometimes we find church-members who, from curiosity or other motives, not unfrequently attend other churches at the time of service in their own. In most such instances no good excuse could be given.

Our church is our religious home; and home should have our preference above all other places. If our love is not perverted, it will, like a true instinct, ever draw us first of all toward our spiritual home as well as our natural home.

Ordinarily, duty points us to our own church. A habit of running hither and thither must cause spiritual dissipation. We shall in more than one way wrong our own hearts. Moreover, our example cannot have due weight. At our own church, where we should be regularly expected, our example will most loudly speak. At other places, where we are not expected, or perhaps little known, we may get the credit for little else than itching ears.

Still further, it is to your spiritual home that you especially owe your powers for doing good. The strength and prosperity of your church must depend, instrumentally, upon its members. There you owe your labor, your presence, your manifested interest. Your own family look to you. Some young or weak fellow church-member may, because of your wandering, be discouraged or learn likewise to wander. Your pastor's heart will grow heavy and his hands will be weakened. Wrong must ever beget wrong. Go to your own church when its doors are open.—*S.*

Early Training in Piety.

As a child is taught to speak, so should he be taught to pray by his mother, and so soon as he can utter his first words to man should his mother lead him to speak to God. Convinced that a child's words reach the heart of God, she will reverently fulfill this maternal duty. When she is making her child say his morning and evening prayer, she is performing a no less sacred and sublime office than the minister of Christ, when, standing at the altar, he sends up to God the prayers of the Church. When story-telling and the earliest instructions begin, the mother should not delay to tell the child stories from the Bible, and especially from the history of the Saviour, in that childish language which none so well understand as a mother. Who can sufficiently pity those parents who suffer themselves to be deprived of so pure a joy as giving to their child the first tidings of his Redeemer, and witnessing the first fresh deep impression made upon a childish mind by these tidings? There is nothing in the world that can compare in the wealth of moral elements of education, and of deepest truths under forms most easy of apprehension, with what we possess for our children in the Bible history.— *Thiersch.*

Doing Good.

The sphere of usefulness to which we are summoned is limited only by the extent of our ability. Certainly, God has not prescribed a limit, either in His word or by general consequences. The command to do good is restricted, on the one hand, only by our own power, and, on the other, by the necessities and wants which surround us. No embargo has been laid upon age, sex, condition, climate, country or color. Far as the wants of man extend, so far extends the benevolence of our Father in heaven, and so far and to so many particulars should our benevolence extend. If the inquiry be made, in what form and in what direction shall we do good? The reply is, in every form and direction which the occasion requires, both for the soul and the body. Some persons conceive that they can be more useful in one place, and in one form of activity, than in another. Let every one be fully persuaded in his own mind, and be certain that he is animated by the spirit of his Divine Master. As the followers of Christ, members of His body, animated by His spirit, the object at which we should aim is the same which brought Him down from heaven to earth—the salvation of the soul. Everything which contributes to the attainment of this end is of the first importance, and should claim the first and undivided attention.—*H. L. Baugher, D. D.*

Wills.

Many Christians, after giving liberally to the Lord during the time of their active life in the world, still further remember the various objects of benevolence when they come to make final disposition of their property in giving form to their last will and testament. We have in our Church many such objects, which are loudly calling for the exercise of liberality. Among them are our Colleges and Theological Seminaries, and our Boards of Home and Foreign Missions, Church Extension, Publication, the Education Society, etc., etc. Here is abundant room for thousands upon thousands of the means which have been put into the hands of Christ's people. Dear Christian friends, make this a subject of sincere and fervent prayer, that you may be rightly directed as your Lord's stewards. And yet one more hint. Some persons have been known not to have exercised proper precaution when making their wills. They have failed to insert the real or corporate names of institutions, boards, etc. Be always careful to secure the exact, lawful name from some officer or other competent person. Such care will secure your property against danger of mistake or diversion.—*S.*

ICELAND.—The one-thousandth anniversary of the settlement of Iceland was celebrated on the 2nd day of August, 1874. Religious services were held with reference to the occasion in the three hundred Lutheran churches of the island

True Wisdom.

Count Axel Oxenstierna was the Chancellor of Sweden under the great king Gustavus Adolphus. He managed the government while the king was abroad in Germany subduing the enemies of religious liberty. When the king's death occurred, the direction of the affairs of state was chiefly placed in his hands until Christina should arrive at a proper age to be crowned. Oxenstierna was not only a wise statesman, but a sincere Christian. He did much to advance the cause of true religion. On one occasion he thus addressed Mr. Whitelock, an English ambassador:

"You are now in the prime of your age and vigor, and in great favor and business; but all this will leave you, and you will one day better understand and relish what I say. You will then find that there is more wisdom, truth, comfort, and pleasure in retiring and in turning your heart from the world to the Spirit of God, and in reading the Bible, than in all the courts and favors of princes."

The Sunday-School.

This blessed cause is awakening increased interest among Christians from year to year. In our own Church there is far more time given to it than formerly in our Synods. In our General Synod, amidst all the pressing duties, it has now cheerfully accorded to it a portion of the precious time. A number of conventions have been held in our Church, within the past year or two, for the purpose of giving special consideration to this department of Christian interest. Besides these gatherings of a more local kind, two general, or national, Lutheran Sunday-School Conventions have been held since the last meeting of the General Synod. The first of these assembled at Bucyrus, Ohio, in November, 1873; and the second at Johnstown, Pennsylvania, in October, 1874. Both these meetings were largely attended by pastors, teachers, and friends. The addresses, essays and discussions were highly instructive. God will add His blessing.—*S.*

NOTHING TO SPARE.—The fine weather of Sabbath last brought out a large attendance at the city churches, notwithstanding the numbers who have fled to the mountains and the sea. Among those who worshipped at Circular Square was Mrs. Worthington Ryce, whose dress was universally admired. It consisted chiefly of a neat black and white fine-striped summer silk (28 yards at $1.25), trimmed with black lace (18½ yards at $1.62); a lovely bonnet by Mixer ($38 without the flowers, which were left over from last year); and a brooch, with ear-drops to match, of very rich but chaste design ($90). The sermon was in behalf of foreign missions, and Mrs. Ryce weighted the contibution-box when it passed her pew with a fifteen cent scrip. It was all she felt she could afford.—*Congregationalist.*

Life Everlasting.

As eye hath not seen, nor ear heard, neither have entered into the heart of man the things which God hath prepared for them that love Him, no one can adequately express, in the language of mortals, the nature of ever-lasting life. It is enough for us to believe that everlasting life is inexpressi-ble bliss, with which God will eternally bless and glorify the faithful, that they with all the angels may eternally live in Him, and, triumphing over the miseries of the world, may love God without weariness, worship Him without satiety, and behold Him without end.—*Dr. L. Hutter, d.* 1616.

Love to God.

Our love to God, through Christ, sanctifies all other loves, as the conju-gal, the filial, the parental, the love of country; because it strips off from the merely human all selfishness, and gratefully recognizes in all the bless-ings of life the highest good. It sanctifies every station, from that of the peasant to that of the king, as well pleasing to God, and moves every one to right actions in the calling which God gives him, and in the position he occupies; be that station high or low, be it one of rank or of poverty. It nerves him to good works—acts which shall receive, from the paternal goodness of God, their promised reward. These are the proper good works, the works of new obedience, which are the consequences of justify-ing faith. They are the good fruit of the noble tree.—*Dr. Ernest Sartorius.*

Religions of the World.

It is difficult to be accurate in figures of this kind, but we can try to approximate. According to the latest estimates, we present the following populations:—

Counted as Christians.

Protestants (of whom from 40,000,000 to 50,000,000 are Lutherans)............106,000,000	
Greeks (or Greek Church)............. 82,000,000	
Romanists........................... 201,000,000	
	389,000,000

Others.

Jews.................................	10,000,000
Mohammedans.........................	160,000,000
Pagans...............................	818,000,000
Population of the World..............	1,377,000,000

PARENTAL EXAMPLE.—Every parent is like a looking-glass for his chil-dren to dress themselves by. Therefore, parents should take care to keep the glass bright and clear, not dull and spotted, as their good example is a rich inheritance for the rising generation.

Living or not Living.

Many whose lives appear to have been shortest, are destined to live the longest. As a man's life consists not in the abundance of his possessions, so also his age, according to the celestial arithmetic, consists not in the number of his days or years. One may have lived an hundred years, and yet not have lived at all. For all the good he has done to himself and others, he might as well have been a stone. He has left no enduring footprints behind; his life has been a failure, a blank. As "the child is father of the man"—as the virtues or vices that rule in youth are apt to control in mature manhood, so, also, the character we form in this life will follow us in the life to come. If we plough iniquity and sow wickedness, verily we shall reap the same.—*Rev. Daniel Garver.*

Godliness.

Godliness has a promise both for this life and for that which is to come. The child of God, under all of the sorrows of life, has a sure refuge. He knows that all things are working together for his good; that not one hair of his head shall perish unknown to his Heavenly Father. In the blessings of life, he sees them as links in an unbroken chain of divine love, and even temporal mercies afford to him an intenser satisfaction than they afford to the unbeliever. When trials come, he knows in whom he can find strength. When he thinks on his earthly future, he feels: "My times are in thy hand," and he would not wish for better keeping. As thoughts of eternity come, he beholds vista after vista of unearthly, unutterable, unfading bliss, stretching beyond the grave. He shall be with God, he shall enjoy God, he shall be like God.

The Lock.

A lock was shown to Gotthold, constructed of rings which were severally inscribed with certain letters, and could be turned round until the letters represented the name Jesus. It was only when the rings were disposed in this manner that the lock could be opened. The invention pleased him beyond measure, and he exclaimed, "Oh that I could put such a lock as this upon my heart!" Our hearts are already locked, no doubt, but generally with a lock of quite another kind. Many need only to hear the words gain, honor, pleasure, riches, revenge, and their hearts open in a moment; whereas to the Saviour and His holy name they continue shut. May the Lord Jesus engrave His name with His own finger upon our hearts, that they may remain closed to worldly joy and worldly pleasure, self-interest, fading honor, and low revenge, and open only to Him!—*Scriver.*

Lutherans in the World.

There are three millions of Lutheran population in Sweden, one and one-half millions in Norway, two millions in Denmark, the Faroe Islands, Iceland and Greenland; one million in France, twenty-five millions in the various Germanic States and principalities, five millions in Prussia, though by State enactment mostly conjoined in one national church with the Reformed; one and one-half millions in Austria, Hungary, Bohemia and Moravia; one million or more in Poland and Russia, one and one-half millions in the United States and Canada, one million in the West India Islands and Australasia, one-half a million in Brazil and other parts of South America, besides large Lutheran populations and churches in other regions and localities. These would run up to some *forty or fifty millions* in all.

The readers may have already learned that their church is the largest Protestant denomination in the world—about as large as all the rest put together. Your church is also established in more countries, and preaches the Gospel in more languages, than can be claimed for any other Protestant church. No church in the world can lay claim to so much learning and authorship as yours can. Christians of all other names are every day learning from the books and lips of her learned men. She can point to thousands of men and women who have been eminent for piety and zeal not surpassed anywhere else. The record of her missionaries and martyrs, who have labored and suffered for Jesus and His Gospel, is admired and cherished the world over.

These things should not make you proud or boasting, but thankful that the Lord has given you a place in this great and good church. Learn to love your church, and cling to her as long as you live. Show by a pure and active life that her teachings are the holy truths of the Bible; and by such a life you will honor the Lord of the church and confer blessings on men.

ABIDING CONFIDENCE.—In the last will and testament of Dr. Martin Luther, the eminent Reformer, occurs the following remarkable passage:—"Lord God, I thank Thee, for that Thou hast been pleased to make me a poor and indigent man upon the earth. I have neither house, nor land, nor money, to leave behind. Thou hast given me wife and children, whom I now restore to Thee. Lord, nourish, teach, and preserve them, as Thou hast me." May many hearts now be inspired by this prominent example of unwavering faith in the Lord!

"THIS Commandment, then, of *love* is both a short commandment and a long commandment; it is a single commandment and many commandments; it is no commandment and all the commandments."—*Luther.*

He Doeth all Things Well.

A little girl was one day working at her worsted—and children should be taught to be busy at something, even though it be but play. A stranger came into the parlor, and, as he looked at her, said, with an apparent sneer: "My dear, what is that you are doing? I see nothing but tangled webs and confused knots.". She looked up archly into his face, and replied: "You are looking on the wrong side: look at the right side;" and she turned it over, and there it was, a beautiful figure of a flower. Oh! my friends, how confused we are, just looking on the wrong side! When God takes us up higher, where the apostle stood when he said, "Nothing shall be able to separate us from the love of God," and we can look down on the right side, then we shall see the lines of beauty, harmony, and sweetness; and when we join the immortal throng,

"This note above the rest shall swell,
My Saviour hath done all things well."

FEVER AND AGUE.—A certain writer maintains that the miasma occasioning this disease may be rendered harmless by cultivating, between the marsh and the dwelling, a belt of sunflowers, hops, or any other high plant which will be growing vigorously at the season when the vegetable decay in the low grounds commences, and thus absorb and utilize the poison.

"WHEN mother says *No*, there's no *Yes* in it." Here's a sermon in a nutshell. Multitudes of parents say "No," but after a good deal of teasing and debate, it finally becomes "Yes." Love and kindness are essential elements in the successful management of children; but firmness, decision, inflexibility, and uniformity of treatment are no less important.

A CLEAR REASON.—The reason why we find so many dark places in the Bible is, for the most part, because there are so many dark places in our hearts. It belongs to the nature of this Book, that it was written for all men of every time, and for all the experiences of each single human heart.—*Dr. Tholuck.*

THERE are many fruits which never turn sweet until the frost has lain on them. There are many nuts that never fall from the boughs of the forest trees until the frost has opened and ripened them. And there are many elements of life that never grow sweet and beautiful until sorrow touches them.

MYSTERY.—In the mysteries of religion, for well-regulated minds, there is always to be found an explanation sufficient for faith, but never as much as is necessary for comprehension. The *what it is* is sufficient for us; but the *how* is beyond our comprehension, and is not at all necessary for us.—*Leibnitz.*

Statistical View of the Evangelical Lutheran Church in North America.

DISTRICT SYNODS IN THE GENERAL SYNOD OF THE U. S. OF AMERICA.

SYNODS.	Ministers.	Churches.	Communicants.
1. Synod of New York and New Jersey	36	45	5,249
2. Hartwick Synod, (N. Y.)	35	32	4,600
3. Franckean Synod, (N. Y.)	24	33	3,243
4. Synod of East Pennsylvania	62	86	11,675
5. Susquehanna Synod	32	54	5,744
6. Synod of West Pennsylvania	61	111	14,877
7. Synod of Central Pennsylvania	31	85	7,589
8. Alleghany Synod, (Penn)	48	110	8,477
9. Pittsburg Synod, (Penn.)	25	50	3,679
10. Synod of Maryland	70	86	14.800
11. German Synod of Maryland	10	14	4,600
12. East Ohio Synod	49	83	6,400
13. Wittenberg Synod, (Ohio)	40	48	4,810
14. Miami Synod, (Ohio)	25	49	3,513
15. Synod of Northern Indiana	39	73	3,910
16. Olive Branch Synod, (Ind.)	16	35	1,570
17. Synod of Northern Illinois	38	67	3,840
18. Synod of Southern Illinois	18	28	1,350
19. Synod of Central Illinois	39	43	3,323
20. Synod of Iowa	23	35	1,100
21. Synod of Kansas	30	29	780
22. Synod of Nebraska	8	20	1,200
23. Swedish Ansgari Synod	10	12	700
	769	1,228	117,029

DISTRICT SYNODS IN THE GENERAL COUNCIL IN AMERICA.

	Ministers.	Churches.	Communicants.
1. New York Ministerium	73	70	24,128
2. Synod of Pennsylvania	170	344	71,785
3. Pittsburg Synod, (Penn.)	55	120	10,800
4. English District Synod of Ohio	26	58	5,800
5. Synod of Indiana	14	39	1,900
6. Synod of Michigan	20	33	4,110
7. Swedish Augustana Synod, (N. West)	93	211	30,127
8. Synod of Texas	27	25	3,200
9. Synod of Canada	21	57	5,000
10. Holston Synod, (Tenn.)	11	25	2,100
	510	982	158,950

DISTRICT SYNODS IN THE (SOUTHERN) GENERAL SYNOD IN NORTH AMERICA.

	Ministers.	Churches.	Communicants.
1. Synod of Virginia	27	58	3,671
2. Synod of South-Western Virginia	21	40	2,298
3. Synod of South Carolina	32	45	4,911
4. Synod of Georgia	11	14	1,009
5. Synod of Mississippi	10	12	910
	101	169	12,799

DISTRICT SYNODS IN THE SYNODICAL CONFERENCE OF NORTH AMERICA.

	Ministers.	Churches.	Communicants.
1. Joint Synod of Missouri, &c., (5 Districts)	525	670	98,000
2. Joint Synod of Ohio, (3 Districts)	161	256	34,300
3. Synod of Illinois	30	37	4,500
4. Synod of Wisconsin	65	128	28,000
5. Synod of Minnesota	25	63	5,100
6. Synod for Norwegian Luth. Ch. in Am.	102	391	49,663
	908	1,545	219,563

SYNODS.	Ministers.	Churches.	Communicants.
1. Synod of Iowa (German)..................109		183	13,000
2. Tennessee Synod............................ 21		68	6,500
3. Synod of North Carolina................ 19		41	4,201
4. Evg. Luth. Synod in America, (Eielsen's). 22		100	6,000
5. Buffalo Synod, Grabau's, (N. Y.)....... 12		15	1,550
6. Buffalo Synod, No. 2 9		13	1,470
7. Concordia Synod, (Virginia)............ 5		23	1,250
8. Conference for Nor. Dan. Luth. Ch. in Am. 50		195	11,000
9. Swedish Ev. Luth. Mission Syn.(N.West). 10		14	910
10. Norwg. Danish Aug'stana Synod,(N.West) 14		43	5,550
	271	695	51,531
00. Danish Church in America................. 9		20	1,500

Gr'd Tot'l—54 Syn.; 2,568 Ministers; 4,639 Churches; 561,372 Communic'ts.

DEATHS OF LUTHERAN MINISTERS.

NAME.	PLACE.	DATE.	AGE.
Krause, C. G. T...............	Faribault, Minn	Oct. 9, 1873.	30y.11m.18d.
Svenson, Jonas.................	Andover, Ill..........	Dec. 21, 1873.	45y. 4m. 4d.
Ritz, Solomon.....	Osnaburg. Ohio	Jan. 7, 1874.	64y.10m.20d.
Schulze, G....................	Ball's Mills, Pa......	Jan. 9, 1874.	95y. 6m. 9d.
Bittle, D. H., D. D..	Savannah, Ga.........	Jan.14, 1874.	In 55th year.
Houck, W. A..................	Orangeville, S. C...	Jan. 18, 1874.	
Pohlman, H. N., D. D......	Albany, N. Y.........	Jan. 20, 1874.	In 74th year.
Waldron, A.....................	Dansville, N. Y......	Jan. 29, 1874.	38 years.
Lazarus, G. M	Quakertown, Pa.....	Jan. 31, 1874.	34y. 8m. 5d.
Eyer, W. J.....................	Catawissa, Pa.........	Feb. 9, 1874.	71 years.
Wigren, Aug. P...............	Gottenberg,Sweden.	Feb. 19, 1874.	24y. 5m. 5d.
Bachman, J., D.D., LL. D.	Charleston, S. C......	Feb. 24, 1874.	84y. 20d.
Stork, Theophilus, D. D.....	Philadelphia, Pa....	Mar. 28, 1874.	59y. 7m.
Hoffman, F. W......	Shakopee, Minn......	May 14, 1874.	57y.6m. 10d.
Von Rohr, H................ ..	Sanborn, N. Y........	May 15, 1874.	77y. 1m. 18d.
Liesman, H.....................	Newton, Iowa........	June 16, 1874.	43y. 3m. 9d.
Zapf, E.......................	Fayette co., Texas...	June 23, 1874.	30 years.
Burkhardt, A. H..............	Springfield, Ill.......	Aug. 25,1874.	41y. 3m. 5d.
Wert, J. D....................	Palatine, N. Y........	Aug. 29,1874.	36y. 10m. 8d.
Brown, J. H....................	Lewistown, Pa........	Sep. 14, 1874.	In 40th year.
Schladermundt, J.............	New York City......	Oct. 18, 1874.	58y. 4m. 20d.

ECCLESIASTICAL MEETINGS.

The first two bodies meet once, at least, in two years; the other two, once a ear	Organized in the Year.	Place of Next Meeting.	Time of Next Meeting.	Number of Next Meeting.
The General Synod.........	1820	Williamsp't, Pa.	May 26, 1875	27th
General Synod (South) ...	1863	Staunton, Va....	May 25, 1876	10th
General Council.............	1867	Galesburg, Ill...	Oct. 7, 1875	9th
Synodical Conference.......	1872	Cleveland, Ohio.	July 14, 1875	4th

LITERARY AND THEOLOGICAL INSTITUTIONS.

THEOLOGICAL SEMINARIES.

NAME.	LOCATION.	SENIOR PROFESSOR.
THEOL. SEM. OF GEN. SYNOD..	Gettysburg, Pa...	J. A. Brown, D. D.
HARTWICK SEMINARY...........	Hart'k Sem.,N.Y.	Rev. P. Bergstresser.
THEOL. DEPT. MISS'Y INSTITUTE	Selinsgrove, Pa...	H. Ziegler, D. D.
THEOL. DEP. WITTENBERG COL.	Springfield, Ohio.	S. Sprecher, D. D., LL. D.
THEOL. DEP. SW. MIS. INST....	Keokuk, Iowa....	Rev. C. Anderson.
THEOL. DEP. CAPITAL UNIV'Y.	Columbus, Ohio..	Rev. W. F. Lehman.
THEOLOGICAL SEMINARY.........	Philadelphia.......	C. F. Schaeffer, D. D.
THEOL. SEM. GEN. SYN. (S.).	Salem, Va.	Rev. S. A. Repass.
THEOL. SEM. MISSOURI SYNOD.	St. Louis, Mo......	Rev. C. F. W. Walther.
THEOL. SEM. OF GER.IOWA SYN.	Mendota, Ills......	Rev. G. Fritschel.
THEOL. DEP. M. LUTHER COL..	Buffalo, N. Y......	Rev. J. A. A. Grabau.
AUGUSTANA SEMINARY...........	Paxton, Ills.......	T. N. Hasselquist, D. D.
AUGSBURG "	Minneapolis, Minn	Rev. A. Weenaas.
THEOLOGICAL "	St. Sebald, Iowa.	Rev. G. Fritschel.
THEOL. DPT. N. CAR. COL	Mt. Pleasant,N.C.	L. A. Bikle, D. D.

COLLEGES.

NAME.	LOCATION.	PRESIDENT.
PENNSYLVANIA COLLEGE.........	Gettysburg, Pa...	M. Valentine, D. D.
MUHLENBERG "	Allentown, Pa....	F. A. Muhlenberg, D. D.
THIEL "	Greenville, Pa....	Rev. H. W. Roth.
WITTENBERG "	Springfield,·Ohio.	Rev. J. B. Helwig.
CAPITAL UNIVERSITY.............	Columbus, Ohio..	Rev. W. F. Lehman.
ROANOKE COLLEGE...............	Salem, Va.........	D. F. Bittle, D. D.
NORTH CAROLINA COLLEGE	Mt. Pleasant,N.C.	L. A. Bikle, D. D.
NEWBERRY "	Walhalla, S. C...	J. P. Smeltzer, D. D.
CONCORDIA "	Fort Wayne, Ind.	Rev. W. Sihler, Ph. D.
CARTHAGE "	Carthage, Ills.....	Rev. D. L. Tressler.
AUGUSTANA "	Paxton, Ills........	T. N. Hasselquist, D. D.
COLLEGE OF GER. IOWA SYN...	Galena, Ills........	Rev. F. Lutz.
LUTHER COLLEGE	Decorah, Iowa...	Rev. L. Larsen.
NORTH-WESTERN UNIVERSITY..	Watertown, Wis.	Rev. A. F. Ernst.
MARTIN LUTHER COLLEGE.......	Buffalo, N. Y......	Rev. J. F. Winkler.
GERMAN LUTHERAN COLLEGE. .	Rutersville, Tex..	Rev. B. Sickel.

GENERAL BENEVOLENT ORGANIZATIONS, ETC.

NAME.	CORRESPONDING SECRETARY.	RESIDENCE.
PARENT EDUCATION SOCIETY...	Prof. L. H. Croll................	Gettysburg, Pa.
FOREIGN MISSIONARY BOARD...	A. C. Wedekind, D. D.:........	New York City.
HOME " " ...	Rev. J. W. Goodlin............	York, Pa.
HOME MISSION'Y BOARD (Ger.)	Rev. C. A. Schloegel............	Baltimore, Md.
CHURCH EXTENSION BOARD....	Rev. J. W. Goodlin............	York, Pa.
MISS'Y ASS'N, E.STATES(Swed)	Rev. J. A. Dahleen........	Boston, Mass.
CHILDREN'S FOR. MISS'Y SOC...	Rev. J. H. Barclay, (Pres.)...	Baltimore, Md.
BOARD OF PUBLICAT'N (Phil'a)	Martin Buehler, (Treas.).......	Philadelphia, Pa.
COM. OF SYS'C BENEFICENCE...	Rev. F. P. Hennighausen	Baltimore, Md.
PASTORS' FUND TRUST.	L. E. Albert, D. D..............	Germantown, Pa.
LUTH. MIN'S' MUT. INS.LEAGUE	B. Sadtler, D. D. (Treas.)....	Lutherville, Md.
HISTORICAL SOCIETY...........	Prof. C. A. Hay, D. D	Gettysburg, Pa.

ACADEMIES.

Hartwick Seminary	Hart'k Sem.,N.Y.	Rev. J. Pitcher,	*Principal.*
St. Matthew's Academy	New York, N.Y.	Rev. E. Bohm,	"
Lutheran Academy	Newark, N.Y.	Rev. E. F. Giese,	"
Missionary Institute	Selinsgrove, Pa	Rev. P. Born,	"
Swedish Mission Institute	Keokuk, Iowa	Rev. C. Anderson,	"
Maryland Conference Inst.	Mechanicst'n, Md.		
Washington Hall	Trappe, Pa	A. Rambo,	"
Zelienople Academy	Zelienople, Pa.	Rev. J. R. Titzel,	"
Swatara Institute	Jonestown, Pa	Rev. E. J. Koons,	"
Overlea School	Catonsville, Md	Rev.G.W.Ebeling,Ph.D.	"
Tableau Seminary	Emlenton, Pa	Rev. J. B. Fox,	"
Institute of District Synod.	Germantown, O.	Rev. J. P. Hentz,	"
Preparat'y Sch'l of Mo. Syn	Springfield, Ill.	G. Kroening,	"
Teachers' Seminary	Addison, Ill	Rev. J.C.W. Lindemann,	"
St. Ansgar Academy	St. Peter, Minn'a.	J. J. Frodeen,	"
Marshall "	Marshall, Wis	Rev. John J. Anderson,	"
Stoughton "	Stoughton, Wis		
Holden "	Holden, Minn'a	T. Jesme,	"
Preparatory School of Col.	Red Wing, Minn.		
Mosheim Institute	Blue Spr'gs,Tenn.	Rev. J. M. Wagner,	"

FEMALE SEMINARIES.

Lutherville Seminary	Lutherville, Md	Rev. J. R. Dimm,	*Principal.*
Hagerstown "	Hagerstown, Md.	John McCron, D. D.	"
Burkittsville "	Burkittsville, Md.	Rev. W. C. Wire,	"
Mt. Pleasant "	Mt. Pleasant,N.C.	Rev. W. E. Hubbert,	"
Staunton "	Staunton, Va	Rev. J. I. Miller,	"
Female College	Marion, Va	Rev. J. J. Scherer,	"
Young Ladies' Institute	St. Josephs, Mo	Rev. C. Martin, M.D.	"
High School (Ger.)	St. Louis, Mo	A. C. Burgdorf,	"

ELEEMOSYNARY INSTITUTIONS.

Orphans' Home (Gen. Synod)	Loysville, Pa	Rev. P. Willard,	*Director.*
Orphans' Farm Sch'l (Boys')	Zelienople, Pa	W. A. Passavant, D. D.	"
Orphans' Home (Girls')	Rochester, Pa	Miss Elizabeth Hupperts,	"
Wartburg Orphans' School.	Mt. Vernon, N.Y.	Rev. C. G. Holls,	"
Emmaus Institute	Middletown, Pa	W. A. Croll,	"
Orphans' Home (Gen. Coun.)	Germantown, Pa.	Rev. G. F. Gartner,	"
" " (Ger.Io. Syn)	Toledo, Ohio	Rev. K. Beckel,	"
" "	Buffalo, N.Y.	Rev. C. Volz,	"
" "	Jacksonville, Ill.	W. A. Passavant, D. D.	"
" " (Swedish)	Vasa, Minn'a	Rev. E. Norelius,	"
" "	St. Louis, Mo	F. W. Ude,	"
" " (Mo. Synod)	Boston, Mass	F. E. A. Senne,	"
" " and Deaf Inst.	Royal Oak, Mich	Rev. G. Speckhardt,	"
" Asylum(Ger.Io.Syn)	Andrew, Iowa	Rev. J. Rembold,	"
" House	Addison, Ill	Rev.Prof.A.G.G.Franke,	"
" " (Scandinav'n)	Andover, Ill	Rev. A. Anderson,	"
Asylum for Aged Pastors.	Burlington, Iowa.	Under Missouri Synod.	
Infirmary	Pittsburg, Pa	W. A. Passavant, D. D.	"
"	Milwaukee, Wis.	W. A. Passavant, D. D.	"
Lutheran Hospital	St. Louis, Mo	F. W. Schuricht,	"
" "	Fort Wayne, Ind.		
Immigrant Mission (Ger.)	New York, N.Y.	Rev. W. Berkemeier,	"
" " (Ger.)	New York, N.Y.	Rev. S. Keyl,	"
" " (Ger.)	Baltimore, Md	W. Sallmann,	"
" " (Nor.)	New York, N.Y.	P. Larsen,	"
" " (Dan.)	New York, N.Y.	Rev. A. B. J. Soeholm,	"

PERIODICAL PUBLICATIONS.

NAME.	WHERE PUBLISHED.	EDITOR.
1. *The Lutheran Observer, (*English*)	Philadelphia, Pa.	Rev. F. W. Conrad, D. D.
2. *The Luth. and Missionary, "	" "	Rev. J. A. Seiss, D. D.
3. *The American Lutheran, "	York, Pa...........	Rev. P. Anstadt.
4. *The Lutheran Visitor, "	Charleston, S C..	Rev. T. W. Dosh, D. D.
5. *Our Church Paper, "	New Market, Va..	Rev. Prof. W. E. Hubbert.
6. *The Lutheran Standard, "	Columbus, Ohio..	Rev. Prof. M. Loy.
7. ‡The Luth. S. School Herald, "	Philadelphia, Pa.	Rev. M. Sheeleigh.
8. ‡The Busy Bee, "	" "	Rev. W. A. Schaeffer.
9. ‡The Sunday-School, "	New Market, Va...	A. L. Henkel.
10. ‡The Luth. Home Monthly, "	Philadelphia, Pa.	Rev. F. W. Conrad, D. D.
11. ‡The Teachers' Journal, "	York, Pa..........	Rev. P. Anstadt.
12. ‡The Morning Star, "	Lancaster, Pa.....	Rev. B. C. Suesserott.
13. ‡Augsburg Lesson-Leaves, "	Philadelphia, Pa.	Committee.
14. ‡Sunday-School Leaves, "	Fort Wayne, Ind.	Rev. S. Wagenhals.
15. ‡Children's Comments, "	York, Pa.........	Rev. P. Anstadt.
16. ¶The Quarterly Review, "	Gettysburg, Pa...	Rev. Prof. J.A. Brown,D.D.
17. ₰The Lutheran Almanac, "	Baltimore, Md....	Rev. M. Sheeleigh.
18. ₰The Church Almanac, "	Philadelphia, Pa.	Rev. Prof. H. E. Jacobs.
1. *Der Luth. Kirchenfreund, (*Ger'n*)	Baltimore, Md....	Rev. R. C. Beer.
2. †Der Lutheraner, "	St. Louis, Mo.....	Rev. Prof. C.F.W.Walther.
3. †Die Luth. Kirchen-Zeitung, "	Columbus, Ohio..	Rev. Prof. W. F. Lehmann.
4. †Der Lutherische Herold, "	New York, N. Y.	Rev. G. F. Krotel, D. D.
5. †Das Kirchenblatt, "	NewHamb'g,Ont.	Rev. C. F. W. Rechenberg.
6. †Evang. Luth. Gemeindeb'tt, "	Milwaukee, Wis..	Rev. R. Adelberg.
7. †Das Kirchenblatt, "	Mendota, Ill.......	Rev. Prof. G. Fritschel.
8. ‡Der Sonntagsgast, "	New York, N. Y.	Rev. G. U. Wenner.
9. ‡Kirchliches Informatorium, "	Detroit, Mich......	Rev. J. Mueller.
10. ‡Die Wachende Kirche, "	Buffalo, N. Y......	Rev. Prof. J. A. A. Grabau.
11. ‡Lehre und Wehre, "	St. Louis, Mo......	Rev. Prof. C. F.W.Walther.
12. ‡Evang. Luth. Schulblatt, "	" "	Rev. J. C. W. Lindemann.
13. †Der Kinder-Garten, "	Chicago, Ills.......	Rev. J. D. Severinghaus.
14. ‡Lutherisches Kinderblatt, "	Pittsburg, Pa.....	Rev. J. P. Beyer.
15. †Der Jugend-Freund, "	Allentown, Pa...	Rev. S. K. Brobst.
16. *Die Lutherische Zeitschrift, "	" " ...	" "
17. *Der Pilger, "	Reading, Pa......	Rev. J. J. Kuendig.
18. ‡Philadelphia Kirchenbote, "	Philadelphia, Pa.	Rev. J. Vogelbach.
19. ‡Lutherisches Volksblatt, "	Elmira, Ontario..	Rev. A. Ernst.
20. ‡Jung-Männer-Bote, "	New York, N. Y.	Cand. E. Bohm.
21. †Die Abendschule, "	St. Louis, Mo.....	Rev. Prof. C. J. H. Fick.
22. ‡Blätter aus dem Waisenhause, "	Andrew, Iowa....	Rev. J. Rembold.
23. ₰Der Lutherische Kalender, "	Allentown, Pa....	Rev. S. K. Brobst.
24. ₰Amerikanischer Kalender, "	St. Louis, Mo......	Rev. C. W. Lindemann.
1. *Evan. Luth. Kirketidende, (*Nor'n*)	Decorah, Iowa....	College Professors.
2. ††Luth. and Missionsbladet, "	Minneapolis, Min.	Rev. Prof. A. Weenaas.
3. ‡Budbäreren, "	Chicago, Ills.......	Rev. J. Z. Torgersen.
1. ‡Zion's Baner, (*Swedish*)	Keokuk, Iowa.....	Rev. Prof. C. Anderson.
2. †Augustana, "	Rock Island	Rev. T. N. Hasselquist, D.D.
3. ‡Missions Vännen, "	Chicago, Ills.......	A. W. Hedenschoug.
4. ‡Barn-Vännen, "	New York, N. Y..	Rev. A. Hult.
1. ‡Kirkelig Samler, (*Danish*)	Racine, Wis........	Rev. Adam Dan.

* Weekly.   † Semi-Monthly.   ‡ Monthly.   ‖ Bi-Monthly.   ¶ Quarterly.   ₰ Yearly.

CLERICAL REGISTER.

List of Names and Post Office Address of Lutheran Ministers in the U. S.

Those having a * prefixed are connected with the **General Synod.**

☞ *Ministers and others are respectfully requested to advise the Publisher of this Almanac of any errors or omissions they may discover in the following list.*

Aas, C C, White Water, Walworth co, Wis.
Aaseroed, P A, Fort Dodge, Webster co, Iowa.
Abele, J G, Lockport, Niagara co, N Y.
Abelson, H W, Norway, La Salle co, Ills.
Achenbach, W. Venedy, Washington co, Ills.
Achilles, J, N St. Louis, Mo.
Acker, H'y, Ottawa, La Salle co, Ills.
Adam, C, jr, Woodland, Barry co, Mich.
*Adams, J A, Mt Carmel, North'd co, Pa.
Ade, J G, Mendota, La Salle co, Ills.
Adelberg, R, Milwaukee, Wis.
Ahlquist, L P, Lincoln, Nebraska.
Ahner, F A, E. Saginaw, Saginaw co, Mich.
Ahner, G E, Nicollet, Nicollet co, Minna.
*Albert, Chas S, Carlisle, Cumberland co, Pa.
Albert, J, Watsontown, North'd co, Pa.
*Albert, Luther E, DD, Germant'n, Phil'a, Pa.
Albrecht, C. Miamisburg, Montgom'y co, Ohio.
Albrecht, J L, Rockford, Wright co, Minna.
Aldrich, N, Vandalia, Fayette co, Ills.
Allsen, A O, Oslo, Manitowoc co. Wis.
Alleman, B F, Shippensb'g, Cumberl'd co, Pa.
*Alleman, M J, York, York co, Pa.
Allwardt, H A, Lebanon, Dodge co, Wis.
Althoff, C, Menomonee, Dunn co, Wis.
Althoff, C H, Greenville, Darke co, Ohio.
Althoff, F W, Springfield, Clark co, Ohio.
*Altman, D S, Ottawa, Franklin co, Kansas.
Amble, O, Gowen, Montcalm co, Mich.
Amlund, N, Story City, Story co, Iowa.
Amonsen, —, Rochester, Olmsted co, Minna.
Andersen, O C, Clinton, DeWitt co, Ills.
Andersen, R, Waupaca, Waupaca co, Wis.
Anderson, A, Vasa, Goodhue co, Minn.
*Anderson, Prof C, Ed "Z Baner," Keokuk, Ia.
*Anderson, G W, Uniontown, Carroll co, Md.
Anderson, Prof J J, Marshall, Wis.
Anderson, L, Norseland, Nicollet co, Minna.
Anderson, N, E. Calumet, Houghton co, Mich.
Andreen, A, Swedona, Mercer co, Ills.
Andrewson, Ole, Leland, La Salle co, Ills.
Angle, H W, M D, Grove City, Christian co, Ill.
*Anjou, Prof John, Galesburg, Ills.
Ansorge, B J, box 173, Paducah, Ky.
*Anspach, J G, Mifflinburg, Union co, Pa.
*Anspach, J M, Reading, Pa.
*Anstadt, P, Ed "Am Luth," York, Pa.
*Anthes, Peter, Mt Carmel, Clermont co, O.
*Anthony, E M, Biehle, Perry co, Mo.
*Anthony, J B, Minersville, Schuylkill co, Pa.
Apple, B F, Stone Church, North'mpt'n co, Pa.
Arendt, F W M, Fraze, Macomb co, Mich.
Artz, Wm, Salisbury, Rowan co, N C.
Asbjornson, P, Clear Lake, Cerro Gordo co, Ia.
Asperheim, O, Oconomowoc, Waukesha co, Wis
*Atkinson, T W, 330 Walnut st, Phila, Pa.
*Aughe, A H, Newport, Perry co, Pa.
*Aughey, Prof Sam'l. Ph D, Lincoln, Neb.
Aulich, E, Ellisville, Keewaunee co, Wis.
*Aurand, F, Rebersburg, Centre co, Pa.
Ausland, J, St Paul, Minna.
Austin, C D, Raleigh, Smith co, Miss.
Austin, J, Springfield, Effingham co, Ga.
*Axline, And'w, Fairfield, Jefferson co, Iowa.

Baartvedt, A, Morris, Stevens co, Minna.
Baarts, R, La Crosse, Wis.
*Babb, A, Blairsville, Indiana co, Pa.
Bachmann, G, sen, Lewisburg, Preble co, O.
Bachmann, G, jr, Reading, Hamilton co, O.
Baeckstroem, C L, Vermillion, Clay co, Dakota.
Baden, J H, 223 Adelphi st, Brooklyn, N Y.
Badenfeld, F Von, DD, Roxboro', Philad'a, Pa.
Bading, J, 416 Milwaukee st, Milwaukee, Wis.
Baechler, Sam'l, Youngstown, Mahoning co, O.
*Bagley, F H, Brooklyn, N Y.
Bailey, J H, Leesville, Lexington co, S C.
*Baird, C, Mt Carroll, Carroll co, Ills.
*Baker, Ezra K, Kickapoo, Peoria co, Ills.
*Baker, H, Altoona, Blair co, Pa.
Baker, Isaac, Winchester, Shenandoah co, Va.
*Baltzly, J B, Bucyrus, Crawford co, Ohio.
Bangerter, E, Peoria, Peoria co, Ills.
Bansemer, C F, Savannah, Ga.
Barb, Prof J C, Mosheim, Greene co, Tenn.
Barb, J H, Bridgewater, Rockingham co. Va.
*Barclay, Jos H, 239 Lanvale st, Balto, Md.
*Barnett, J N, Constantine, St Joseph co, Mich.
*Barnett, W C, Florence, Boone co, Ky.
*Barnitz, F A, Middletown, Dauphin co, Pa.
*Barnitz, Samuel B, Wheeling, W Va.
Barth, G, Minnesota Lake, Minn'a.
Bartholomew, A H, Davenport, Iowa.
Bartholomew, A N, Leesville, Carroll co, Ohio.
Bartholomew, M M, Goshen, Elkhart co, Ind.
Bartling, W, Chicago, Ills.
*Battersby, G S, Warrior's Mark, Hunt'n co, Pa.
Bauch, J, Oak Harbor, Ottawa co, Ohio.
Bauer, A C, Monroe, Monroe co, Mich.
Bauer, Ernest A, Hazleton, Luzerne co, Pa.
Bauer, Henry, Wapakonetta, Auglaize co, Ohio.
Bauermeister, W G C, Stendal, Pike co, Ind.
*Baugher, Prof H L, Gettysburg, Adams co, Pa
Baughman, G, sen, Lewisburg, Preble co, O.
Baum, G, Ashland, Boyd co, Ky.
*Baum, W M, DD, 458 n 6th st, Philad'a, Pa.
*Baum, J Croll, Gettysburg, Pa.
Baumann, C, Wilkens, Alleghany co, Pa.
Baumann, G, Chandlersville, Cass co, Ills.
Baumann, J, Freedom, Washtenaw co, Mich.
Baumbach, C, jun, Tripoli, Bremer co, Iowa.
Baumbach, J, sen, W Union, Fayette co, Iowa.
Baumbach, W, Severn Bridge, Mor'n co, Ont.
Baumgaertner, J E, Jonesboro', Union co, Ill.
Baumgart, J P, Warsaw, Hancock co. Ills.
Baumhoefener, C W, Columbus, Nebraska.
Bayer, J F, Tamaqua, Schuylkill co, Pa.
*Bean, A, New Columbia, Massac co, Ills.
Beard, C, Waynesboro', Augusta co, Va.
Bechtel, P, Eberle, Effingham co, Ills.
Beck, C E, St Louis, Mo.
Beck, Jos, Lithopolis, Fairfield co, Ohio.
Beckel, K, East Toledo, Lucas co, Ohio.
Becker, C, Staunton, Macoupin co, Ills.
Becker, F C, Lordstown, Trumbull co, Ohio.
*Becker, G, Perry, Pike co, Ills.
Becker, H A, Thornville, Perry co, Ohio.
*Beckley, G H, Boonsboro', Wash'n co, Md.
Beckman, F W, Humboldt, Nemaha co, Neb.

Beckman, I P, Kandiyohi, Minna.
*Beckner,Dan'l, Mahanoy City, Schuy'l co,Pa.
Bedenbaugh, Z W, Columbia, S C.
Bedenbaugh, L, Senola, Coweta co, Ga.
Bedeubaugh, S W, Lake City, Columbia, Fla.
*Beer, R. C, Ed " Luth Kirch'd," Balto, Md.
*Behm, Ernst, Jacksonville, Morgan co, Ills.
*Beidler, J A, Twin Grove, Green co, Wis.
Belfour, E, 185 Huron st, Chicago, Ills.
Bell, J A, St Clair's Bottom, Va.
*Bell, Lewis J, Smithsburg, Wash Co, Md.
*Bell, P G, Polo, Ogle co, Ills.
*Belmer, H B, Sclinsgrove, Snyder co, Pa.
Belser, H F, N Washington,Crawford co, Ohio.
Bender, C, Red Wing, Minna.
*Benedict, F, Bedford, Bedford co, Pa.
Bensen, T, Springfield, Ills.
Benzon, J S, Omaha, Neb.
Bennick, J S, Forestville, Shenandoah, Va.
Benze, A L, Erie, Pa.
Benzin, C F L, Salamonia, Jay co, Ind.
*Berg, A, Chambersburg, Franklin co, Pa.
Berge, N, New Hope, Portage co, Wis.
Bergen, J, Jacksonville, Morgan co, Ills.
*Bergenskoeld, N G, Beattie, Kan.
Berggren, C H L, Elgin, Kane co, Ills.
Berggren, C O, Warren, Warren co, Pa.
Bergh, A, Ole, Fergus Falls, Minna.
Bergh, J E, Minnesota Crossing, Minna.
Bergh, Prof K, Decorah,Winneshiek co, Iowa.
Hergh, O A, Byron, Olmsted co, Minn.
Bergholz, W, Clifton, Monroe co, Wis.
*Bergstresser, Prof P, Hartwick Seminary, Otsego co, N Y.
Bergt, A W, Uniontown, Perry co, Mo.
Berkemeier, W, Mt Vernon,W Chester co, N Y.
Berkemeyer, F, Sellersville, Bucks co, Pa.
Berner, Chas L, Horicon, Dodge co, Wis.
Berner, U, Harlemville, Columbia co, N Y.
Bernheim, C H, Lexington, Davidson co, NC.
Bernheim, G D, Wilmington N C.
Bernreuther, J, Olean, Cattaraugus co, N Y.
Bernthal, G, Richville, Tuscola co, Mich.
Berntzon, S, Colfax, Dunn co, Wis.
Beroset, A, Archbold, Fulton co, Ohio.
Berry, B F, Midway, Barnwell co, S C.
*Berry, E E, Northumberland, Pa.
Besel, F C, Cape Girardeau, Mo.
Bethke, H, Rochester, Fulton co, Ind.
*Betz, C, New Bremen, Auglaize co, Ohio.
Beuze, A L, Erie, Pa.
Beyer, J P, Pittsburgh, Pa.
Bickel, H M, Centre Sq're, Montgom'y co, Pa.
*Biddle, F, Zanesville, Wells co, Ind.
*Biddle, J G, Elkhart, Elkhart co, Ind.
Bieber, I W, Bethlehem, Northampton co, Pa.
Biedermann, R H, Cincinnati, Ohio.
Biewend, A, 19 Dell Ave, Boston, Mass.
Bikle, Prof L A, D D, Mount Pleasant, N C.
*Bikle, Prof P M, Gettysburg, Pa.
*Billheimer, T C, box 4016, Pittsburg, Pa.
Blitz, F Julius, Concordia, Lafayette co, Mo.
Birch, A, Lake, Stark co, Ohio.
Bischoff, Prof R A, Fort Wayne, Ind.
Bittle, Prof D F, DD, Salem, Roanoke co, Va.
Bjarnason, Prof Jon, Decorah, Iowa.
Bjoerge, K K, Lake Park, Becker co, Minna.
Bjork, C A, Mineral Ridge, Boone co, Iowa.
Bjorn, B J, Oslo, Manitowoc co, Wis.
Bjorn, L M, Clark's Mill, Manitowoc co, Wis.
*Black, Geo B, Springfield, Ills.
*Blackwelder, DM,Mifflintown,Juniata co,Pa.
Blessin, G, Denver, Bremer co, Iowa.

Blom, —, Detroit, Dickinson co, Kansas.
*Bloom, J K, Tipton, Cedar co, Iowa.
Blumer, Adam, Edington, Rock Is'd co, Ills.
Bock, C, Houser's Spring, Jefferson co, Mo.
Bockrodt, —, —, Canada.
Bockstahler, J, Liverpool, Onondaga co, N Y.
Bode, C E, Toledo, Lucas co, Ohio.
Bode, C E, Fort Wayne, Ind.
Boden, A F, Kellogg, Jasper co, Iowa.
Boehm, J G, London, Ontario.
Boehme, E A, Union City, Randolph co, Ind.
Boehner, C F, Reed City, Osceola co, Mich.
Boerneke, C, Danville, Blue Earth co, Minn.
Boeling, F, Waldenburg, Macomb co, Mich.
Boesche, F, Watertown, Carver co, Minn.
Boese, C, Defiance, Ohio.
Boettger, A, Eggertsville, Erie co, N Y.
Boetticher, J T, Mt Pulaski, Logan cn, Ills.
Bohn, J A, Rogers City, Presque Isle co,,Mich.
Bolles, E A, Columbia, S C.
*Bolton, V F, Fayette, Seneca co, N Y.
*Bond, J, Beardstown, Cass co, Ills.
Booher, J K, Newark, Licking co, Ohio.
Booher, N, Shannondale, Montgo'y co, Ind.
*Boon, John, Indianapolis, Ind.
Boozer, C P, Springfield, Effingham co, Ga.
Borchard, G, 30 Rector st, New York, N Y.
Borchers, H, Seymour, Jackson co, Ind.
Borge, O M, St Peter, Nicollet co, Minna.
Borgell, O, Decorah, Winneshiek co, Iowa.
Born, P, Rochester, Beaver co, Pa.
*Born, Prof P, Selinsgrove, Snyder co, Pa.
*Borns, J, Springfield, Clark co, Ohio.
Bostad, O, K Lake, Minn.
Both, Victor, Norwich, New London co, Conn.
Bouknight, S, Leesville, Lexington co, S. C.
Bowen, O W, Ligonier, Noble co, Ind.
*Bowers, Geo A, Hillsboro,' Montg'ry co, Ills.
*Bowers, H G, Jefferson, Frederick co, Md.
Bowles, J D, Seneca City, Oconee co, S C.
Bowman, W Spener, D D, Charleston, S C.
Bowman,W A,West Carrollton, Montg'y co, O.
*Boyer, M G, Newry, Blair co, Pa.
Boyer, S R, Lancaster, Pa.
Boyum, A E, Arendahl, Fillmore co, Minna.
Brakhage,W, Bennington, Switzerland co,Ind.
Brammer, H, Lowden, Cedar co, Iowa.
Brand, P, Washington, D C.
*Brandau, G H, Schenectady, N Y.
Brandstetter, G, Golconda, Pope co, Ills.
Brandt, E C E, Baden, St Louis co, Mo.
Brandt, J, Delhi, Norfolk co, Ontario.
Brandt, Prof N, Decorah,Winneshiek co, Iowa.
Brandt, W, Flora, Waterloo co, Ont.
Brater, J J, Pemberville, Wood co, Ohio.
Brauer, A H, Allegheny City, Pa.
Brauer, E A, St Louis, Mo.
Brauer, Prof K, Addison, Dupage co, Ills.
Brauer, Theo, Sherrill's Mt, Dubuque co,Iowa.
Braun, C, Houston, Harris co, Texas.
Braun, F L, Eau Claire, Wis.
Braun, H, Belleplain, Scott co, Minna.
Braun, J L, Monroeville, Allen co, Ind.
Braunwarth, W, Dundee, Monroe co, Mich.
Brecht, C F W, Perrysville, Alleghany co, Pa.
Brecht, F, Burton, Adams co, Ills.
Brecht, G H, Fowler, Adams co, Ills.
Breckenridge, J B, Rochester, Beaver co, Pa.
*Breckenridge, Prof S F, Springfield, Ohio.
Bredesen, A, Leeds, Columbia co, Wis.
Bredow, P, Maxfield, Bremer co, Iowa.
*Breidenbaugh, E, Gettysburg, Adams co, Pa.
*Breitenbach, Prof J W, Gettysburg, Pa.

Breitfeld, F W, Lawrenceb'g, Dearborn co,Ind.
Bremer, H, Lake Creek, Benton co, Mo.
*Breuninger, J G, Muhlenberg Mis'n, Africa.
Brenneman, Isaac, Ridgeway, Elk co, Pa.
Brenner, P, Oshkosh, Winnebago co, Wis.
*Brewer, H M, Litchfield, Montgomery co, Ill.
Brezing, T, Heidelberg, Waterloo co, Ontario.
*Bricker, J K, Stoystown, Somerset co, Pa.
*Bridgman,A L,Argusville, Schoharie co,N Y.
*Bright, J A. Hublersburg, Centre co, Pa.
Brink, N J, Duluth, St Louis co, Minna.
Brobst, S K, Allentown, Lehigh co, Pa.
Brockmann, JH, Ft Atkinson, Jefferson co,Wis
*Brodfuehrer, J C, 185 St Mark's pl, New Y'k.
Broehaug, C O, Esdoile, Pierce co, Wis.
Broemer, A, Paterson, N J.
Brohm, T J, St Louis, Mo.
Brohm, Prof T, Watertown, Jefferson co, Wis.
Brown, A J,DD,Blountsville,Sullivan co,Tenn.
*Brown, A R, Rows, Ashland co, Ohio.
Brown, E, Sterling, Whiteside co, Ills.
Brown, H M, Salisbury, Rowan co, N C.
*Brown, Prof JA, DD, Gettysb'g, Adams co,Pa
Brown, Jas A, Wytheville, Wythe co, Va.
*Brown, O, 378 N Alabama st, Ind'polis, Ind.
Brown, R L, Salisbury, Rowan co, N C.
Brown, W J, St Paul's, Pickaway co, Ohio.
*Brubaker, J, Gettysburg, Adams co, Pa.
*Bruce, S, South Worcester, Otsego co, N Y.
Bruckner, H, Pine Hill, Sanilac co, Mich.
Bruegel, G A, Warren, Warren co, Pa.
Bruer, H, Snipley, Perth co, Ontario.
Brueggemann, F W, Inglefield,Vand'g co,Ind.
Bruegmann, C A, Edwardsv'e, Mad'n co, Ill.
Bruegmann.GGW,Rosselle Stat'n,Dup co,Ills.
Brun, N C, East Norway, Doniphan co, Kans.
Brunning, H H, Ph. D, Erie, Pa.
Bucka, J, ——, Iowa.
Buechle, F, Grafton, Ozaukee co, Wis.
Buchholz, G C E, Middletown, Butler co, O.
Buechler, C, Bellevue, Huron co, Ohio.
Buehring, W, Waterloo, Black Hawk co, Iowa.
Buehl, J P, Massillon, Stark co, Ohio.
Buehler, J, San Francisco, California.
Buehler, W R, Hastings, Westchester co, N Y.
Buehring, H, Algona, Kossuth co, Iowa.
Buerer, M, Lawler, Chickasaw co, Iowa.
Buenger, J F, St Louis, Mo.
Buerger, E M, Hart, Winona co, Minn.
Buerkle, A, Woodville, Sandusky co, Ohio.
Buerkle, M, Findlay, Hancock co, Ohio.
Buermeyer, F F, Wilkesbarre, Luzerne co. Pa.
*Buhrman, A, Lovettsville, Loudon co, Va.
Bull, R R, Manistee, Mich.
Bundenthal, J, Leland, Leelenaw co, Mich.
Burger, Julius G, Staunton, Staunton co, Neb.
*Burgner, J B, Milton, Northumb'd co, Pa.
Burfeind, B, Minonk, Woodford co, Ills.
Burk, M, Buffalo, N Y.
*Burkart, N, Baltimore, Md.
*Burket, J N, Washington, D C.
Burkhardt, G, Weehawken. Hudson co, N J.
Burkhardt, J, Tontogany, Wood Co, Ohio.
*Burkhalter, I C, Lewisburg, Union co, Pa.
Burmester, W, Alpena, Alpena co, Mich.
*Burrell, J I,Stone Church, North'ton, co,Pa.
*Burwick, J, Windsor, Randolph co, Ind.
Busby, Geo W, Lewisburg, Preble co, Ohio.
Bushong, A A J, Arbor Hill, Augusta, Va.
Busse, C, Aurora, Dearborn co, Ind.
Busse, Wm, New York, N Y.
Buszin T, Secor, Woodford co, Ills.
*Butler, J G, DD, 1107 11th st, Wash'n, D C.

Butz, J G, Zelienople, Butler co, Pa.

Caemmerer, A, Mountville, Sibley co, Minna.
*Cain, D F, Monmouth, Adams co, Ind.
Cammerer, H, Decatur, Adams co, Ind.
Campbell, J F, Capon Road Depot, Va.
Camman, D P, Augusta, Richmond co, Ga.
Carlsen, P, Bevens Creek, Carver co, Minna.
Carlsen, E, Box 1252, Chicago, Ills.
Carlson, F H, Ossian, Winneshiek co, Iowa.
Carlson,L A K,Alexandria,Douglass co,Minna
Casa, O, Fergus Falls, Ottertail co, Minna.
*Caskey, C, Ligonier, Noble co, Ind.
Catenhusen, J, Rockville, Mo.
Caughman, E M, Leesville, Lexington co, S C.
Cavallin, J O, White Rock, Goodhue co, Minn.
Cederstam, P A, Mooers' Prairie, Minna.
Cervin, Prof A R, Dr, Rock Island, Ills.
Challman, A, 149 E Chicago ave, Chicago, Ill.
Chilleen, O, Morgan, Clay co. Kan.
Christ, L, Independence, Buchanan co, Iowa.
Christensen,E G A,Gayville,Yank'n co,Dak'a.
Christy,V B,Salem X Roads,Westmorl'd co,Pa
*Clanahan, A H. Golconda, Pope co, Ills.
*Clare, R H, Bridgeton. Cumberland co, N J.
Claus, G R A, Macon City, Mo.
Claus, M, Shelbyville, Shelby co, Ills.
Claussen, C L, St Ansgar, Mitchell co, Iowa.
Cleszler, C. Transfer, Mercer co, Pa.
Cloeter, H, Lakeland, Washington co, Minna.
Cloninger, J, Mouse Creek, McMinn co, Tenn.
*Clutz, J A. 50 McMechen st, Baltimore, Md.
*Coates, C S, Lamertine, Clarion co, Pa.
*Cochel, G Z, Mt Vernon, Knox co, Ohio.
*Collins, B B, Gettysburg, Adams co, Pa.
*Colver, M, Apollo, Armstrong co, Pa.
Compton, G A, Kasson, Barbour co, W Va.
*Conaway, J, York, York co, Pa.
Conder, I, McGaheysville, Rockingham co,Va.
Cone, W H, Gold Hill, Rowan co, N C.
*Conrad, F W, D D, Ed "L Obs," 1928 Spring
  Garden street, Philadelphia, Pa.
Conrad, J, Theresa, Dodge co, Wis.
Conrad R, Jordan, Scott co, Minna.
*Conrad, V L, 524 Walnut st, Philadelphia,Pa
*Conradi, J P, Cumberl'd, Alleghany co, Md.
*Conradi, F A, Oswego, N Y.
*Cook, H S, Newton, Jasper co, Iowa.
*Cook, J J, Millersburg, Elkhart co, Ind.
*Cook, Sam'l, Hastings, Mills co, Iowa.
Cooper, C J, S Bethlehem, Northam. co, Pa.
Cooper, J E, Winchester, Va.
*Copenhaver,A,McAllisterville,Juniata co,Pa
*Corbet, J B, Abilene, Dickinson co, Kansas.
Corbet, T W, Herring, Allen co, Ohio.
Corbes, F A, Central, St Louis co, Mo.
*Cornell, N H,Chester Springs, Chester co,Pa
Cornman, W O, Phillipsburg,Warren co, N J.
Cossman, Carl E, Lunenburg, Nova Scotia.
Cox, G H, Spring Grove, Knox Co, Tenn.
Cramer, Prof A, St Louis, Mo.
Cramer,C A J,Sulphur Springs,Crawford co,O.
Cramer, H G, Zanesville, Logan co, Ohio.
Cramer, Jos, Paulding, Paulding co, Ohio.
Cramer, J L, Waverly, Bremer co, Iowa.
Crantz, D, Winesburg, Holmes co, Ohio.
*Crebs, W E, Wellersburg, Somerset co, Pa.
*Cressler, J F, Apollo, Armstrong co, Pa.
Cressman, J J, S Easton. Northamp'n co, Pa.
*Crigler, A I, Des Moines, Polk co, Iowa.
*Crigler, John J, Nevada, Story co, Iowa.
*Criley, Wm W, Lock Haven, Clinton co,Pa.
*Crist, J B, Altoona, Blair co, Pa.

*Crist, Isaac B, Dale City, Somerset co, Pa.
*Croft, Sam'l, Chambersb'g, Franklin co, Pa.
*Croll, A D, Lyons Station, Berks co, Pa.
*Cromer, A J, Sturgis, St Joseph co, Mich.
*Cromer, Jno B, Irving, Montgomery co, Ills.
Cronenwett, G, Woodville, Sandusky co, O.
Cronenwett, E, Delaware, Ohio.
Crouse, A L, Summit Point, Lexington co, S C
*Crouse, B F, Millersburg, Holmes co, Ohio.
*Crouse, J, Bucyrus, Crawford co, Ohio.
Crouse, T, Sandy Creek, Randolph co, N C.
Crull, Prof A, Fort Wayne, Ind.
*Culler, Isaac, Spring Mills, Richland co, O.
*Culler, J H, Bryan, Williams co, O.
*Culler, M L, Martinsb'g, Berkeley co, W Va.
Cunz, F B, Ellenville, Ulster co, N Y.
Cupp, J H, Brandonville, Preston co, W Va.
Currie, R M, Trenton, Smith co, Miss.
*Curtis, Sylv, Athens, Greene co, N Y.
*Cutter, W I, Meyerstown, Lebanon co, Pa.

*Daering, M. North Amherst, Ohio.
Dageforde, H, Barre Mills, La Crosse co, Wis.
Dahl, J M, Benson Grove, Winnebago co, Ia.
Duhl, T, Fort Howard, Brown co, Wis.
Dahl, T H, Emerald, Farib co, Minna.
*Dahleen, J A, 17 Lagrange st, Boston, Mass.
Dahlen, O O, Wagon Landing, Polk co, Wis.
Dahlke, W, Clayton, Adams co, Ills.
Dahlsten, A W, Salina, Saline co, Kas.
Dalb, J L, Oshkosh, Winnebago co, Wis.
Dale, E O, Jewell Centre, Jewell co, Kansas.
Damm, C, Bloomfield, Walworth co, Wis.
Dammann, L, Liverpool, Medina co, Ohio.
Dammann, W, Milwaukee, Wis.
Damstroem, A, Swede Valley, Iowa.
Damstroem, C J, Moingona, Boone co, Iowa.
Dan, Adam, Racine, Racine co, Wis.
*Daniels, A N, Ancram, Columbia co, N Y.
Dankworth, F, Detroit. Mich.
Darmstaetter, J A, Columbia, Lanc'r co, Pa.
*Daron, E, Harrisburg, Pa.
*Dasher, Solomon. Harrisburg, Pa.
Dautenhahn, C, North Judson, Stark co, Ind.
Davis, Prof J B, D D, Salem, Va.
*Day, D A, Muhlenberg Mission, Africa.
Defendarfer, D L, Zelienople, Butler co, Pa.
Dehlert, G, Fort Madison, Iowa.
Deindorfer, J. Defiance, Ohio.
*Deininger, A G, East Berlin, Adams co, Pa.
*Deininger, C J, York, York co, Pa.
*Deininger, W A, Chenoa, McLean co, Ills.
Deisz, W F, Meadville, Crawford co, Pa.
*Deitzler, J M, Annville, Lebanon co, Pa.
Dejung, J, Des Moines, Polk co, Iowa.
*Delo, Isaiah J, Leetonia, Columbiana co, O.
*Delo, R F, Three Rivers, St Joseph co, Mich.
Demetro, C H, Perryville, Perry co, Mo.
Denke, W, Chicago, Ills.
Denninger, A, Johnson's Creek, Jef'n co, Wis.
Denninger, G, Oakwood, Milwaukee co, Wis.
Derrick, J Noah, Springfield, Effingham co, Ga
Derrick, Paul, Leesville, Lexington co, S C.
Dethlefs, M F, Sharpsburg, Allegheny co, Pa.
*Detweiler. J S, Oregon. Ogle co, Ills.
Detzer, A, Des Plaines, Cook co, Ills.
Detzer, L A. Lynnville, Warrick co, Ind.
Deuber, S, Bremen, Wabashaw co, Minna.
Dewald, J A, New London, Oneida co, N Y.
*Deyoe, Eph, Ramsey's Stat'n, Bergen co, N J.
Dicke, P H, Upham, Shawano co, Wis.
Diederich, Prof H W, Fort Wayne, Ind.
*Diefendorf, C, Seward, Schoharie co, N Y.

*Diehl, C F, Metamora, Franklin co, Ind.
*Diehl, George, DD, Frederick, Md.
Diehl, G, Pella, Shawanaw co, Wis.
*Diehl, S A, Gettysburg, Pa.
Diehlmann, C, Cambria, Columbia co, Wis.
Diehlman, J F, ——, Wis.
Diemer, H, Elkhart, Ind.
*Diener, John F, New Germ'n, Hunt'n, N J.
*Dietrich, J J, Susp'n Bridge, Niag'a co, N Y.
Dietrichson, I L P, Chicago, Ill.
*Dietterich, J F, Dickinson, Cumberland co, Pa.
Dietz, G F, St Donatus, Jackson co, Iowa.
Dillman, G, Wooster, Ohio.
Dillner, P, Litchfield, Meeker co, Minna.
*Dimm, Prof J R, Lutherville, Balto co, Md.
Dingeldey, J, Sidney, Shelby co, Ohio.
Dinkle, W H, Bridgewater, Rockingham co, Va.
*Diven, W H, Salona, Clinton co, Pa.
Dizinger, J C, Camden, N J.
Doederlein, F, Chicago, Ills.
*Doerr, Phil. Cochran's Mills, Armst'ng co, Pa.
Doerfler, J, Bridgewater, Washtenaw co, Mich.
Doering, G, Glencoe, Cook co, Ills.
Doermann, J H, Yorkville, Kendall co, Ills.
Doepken, J A G, Marietta, Washington co, O.
Doering, E. ——, Mo.
Doescher, J F, Ft Dodge, Webster co, Iowa.
Dohler, A G, Altenburg, Perry co, Mo.
*Domer, Samuel, Washington, D. C.
*Donmeyer, J G, Buena Vista, Steph'n co, Ills
Dorn, W, Dunton, Cook co, Ills.
Dornbirer, J, Loudonville, Ashland co, Ohio.
*Dornblaser, T F, Kansas City, Mo.
Dosh, Thos W, D D, Charleston, S C.
*Douglas, A J, Columbia City, Whitley co, Ind.
Dowidat, C, Hika, Manitowoc co, Wis.
*Dox, H L, Gasport, Niagara co, N Y.
*Drake, Thos, Somerset, Perry co, Ohio.
Drees, G W, 172 Wyckoff st, Brooklyn, N Y.
Dreher, Godfr'y, Frog Level, Newberry co, S C.
Dreyer, F, Accident, Alleghany co, Md.
Droegemiller, J, Nokomis, Mont'y co, Ills.
Dubiel, B, Brooklyn, Cuyahoga co, Ohio.
Duborg, H P, S Chicago, Ills.
Dubpernell, F, Wellesley, Waterloo co, Ont.
Duemling. Dr. H, Fort Wayne, Ind.
Duerschner, C, Cairo, Alexander co, Ills.
Dufford, E, Graniteville, Edgefield co, S C.
Dulitz, L, Napoleon, Henry co. Ohio.
*Dunbar, W H, 115 Cattell st, Easton, Pa.
Dunsing, J, Florence, Morgan co, Mo.
*During, M, Plato, Loraine co, Ohio.
*Dustmann, J M, Carey, Wyandot co, Ohio.
*Dutt, Eph, W Fairview, Cumberland co, Pa.
*Duy, J C, Mont Vale, Bergen co, N J.

*Earhart, D, Levansville, Somerset co, Pa.
*Earhart, M G, Pine Grove Mills, Centre co, Pa.
Earley, J W, Pillow, Dauphin co, Pa.
*Earnest, J A, Westminster, Carroll co, Md.
*Earnheart, T, Murphysboro' Jackson co, Ill.
*Ebeling, G W, Ph D, Catonsville, Balt co, Md.
Ebendick, A, College Point, Long Island, N Y
Eberhard, Chris, Saginaw City, Mich.
Ebert, L, Ridgeville, Monroe co, Wis.
Ebert, C F, Hancock, Houghton co, Mich.
*Ebert O F, Mt Pulaski, Logan co. Ills.
Ebsen, H, Waterloo, Seneca co, N Y.
Eckelman, H, Helenville, Jefferson co, Wis.
*Eckman, A K. Osborn City, Neosho co, Kan.
Edgren, A. Aurora, Kane co. Ills.
Efird, Dan'l, Pine Ridge, Lexington co, S C.
Eggen, J M, Orfordville, Rock co, Wis.

Eggerking, F W, LaGrange, Lewis co, Mo.
Eggers, Herman, Carlisle, Cumberland co, Pa.
Eggers, L G, Palmyra. Lebanon co, Pa.
Eggert, F S, Minonk, Woodford co, Ills.
Ehinger, F, Stevensville, Wesland co, Ont.
Ehmke, J, Oconomowoc,Waukesha co,Wis.
*Ehrenfeld, A C, Indiana, Indiana co, Pa.
*Ehrenfeld, Prof C L, Sagamore, Wash'n, Pa.
*Ehrenfeld, G F, Leechburg, Armst'ng co,Pa
Ehrhart, Julius, 263 W 125 st, New Y'k city.
Eichelberger,W, Charlestown, Jefe'n co,WVa.
*Eichholtz, G, Muncy, Lycoming co, Pa.
Eidahl, K O, Mt Morris, Waushara co, Wis.
Eielsen, Elling, 469 W Erie st, Chicago, Ills.
Eipperle, J, Sturgis, St Joseph co, Mich.
Eirich, J C. Homerville, Medina co, Ohio.
Eirich, M, Nashville, Washington co, Ills.
Eirich, P, Albany, N Y.
Eirich, R, Purcell's Station, Knox co, Ind.
*Eisenhauer, A, Bolivar, Ohio.
Eisenlord, J, Ft Plain, Montgomery co, N Y.
Elsteinsen, E, Roland, Story co, Iowa.
Ekermeyer, W; Cove Dale, Hamilton co, O.
Ekstroem, S, Campbello, Mass.
Ellenberger, D, Wooster. Ohio.
Ellestad, N J, Portland, Maine.
*Ellinger, J G, Ottawa, Franklin co, Kan.
Ellingson, Arne, Arendahl, Fillmore co, Minn
Elmore, E, Senoia, Coweta co, Ga.
Elmore, J S, Senoia, Coweta co, Ga.
*Elser, J W, Princeton, Bureau co, Ills.
*Emerick, W H. Catskill, Greene co, N Y.
*Emerson, R D, Samuel's Depot, Nelson co,Ky
Emery, W S, Kintnersville, Bucks co, Pa.
Emmel, L, St. Peter, Nicollet co, Minna.
*Empie, M W,W Sandlake, Rensellaer co, NY.
*Enders, G W, New Chester, Adams co, Pa.
Endeward, W, Berlin, Green Lake co, Wis.
Endres, G, Booue, Boone co, Iowa.
Engdahl, A, Cambridge, Isanti co, Minna.
Engle. A O, 1105 Filbert st, Philadelphia, Pa.
*Engel, S S, Fisherville, Dauphin co, Pa.
Engelbert, W P, Racine, Racine co, Wis.
Engelbrecht, H, Chicago, Ills.
Engelder, C, Pittsburg, Pa.
Engelke, —, ——, Iowa.
Eugers, P, Blair's Corners, Clarion co, Pa.
Eppling, F, Kirchhayn, Washington co, Wis.
*Erb, I N S, Owigsburg, Schuylkill co, Pa.
Erdman. Fred, Red Bud, Randolph co, Ills.
Endahl, G M, Omaha, Nebraska.
*Erick, E W, Spencerville, De Kalb co, Ind.
Erickson, A, ——, Kansas.
Erickson, G, Weydahl, Chippewa co, Minna.
Erickson, P, Chicago, Ills.
Erle, C L, Colley, Sullivan co, Pa.
Erlenmeyer, C G, Freeburg, Snyder co, Pa.
Ermel, G, Houston, Harris co, Texas.
*Ernsberger, CS,Wapakonetta, Auglaize co,O.
Ernst, Aug, Elmira, Ontario.
Ernst, Prof A F,Watertown, Jefferson co,Wis.
Ernst, C W, Providence, R I.
Ernst, F, Burton. Washington co, Texas.
Ernst, H, Blue Island, Cook co, Ills.
*Essick, A, Fort Harker, Ellsworth co, Kans.
Estrem, O O, Clifton, Bosque co, Texas.
Estel, P S, Pierce, Neb.
Evald, C A, Minneapolis, Minna.
*Evans, W P, Gallupville, Schoharie co, N Y.
*Everett,Thos T, Red Hook, Duchess co,N Y.
Evers, H, Bingen, Adams co, Ind.
Everson, E S E, Perth Amboy, Mid'x co, N J.
Ewh, G, Jersey City, N J.

*Exline, G A, Bunker Hill, Lyon co, Kan.
*Exline, V, Vanwert, Vanwert co, Ohio.
*Eyster, W F, Pleasant Hill, Saline co, Neb.

Fackler, J P, Columbia Bottom, Mo.
Fahs, J F, Akron, Summit co, Ohio.
*Fair, M W, York. Pa.
Fairchild, H, Lovely Dale, Knox co, Ind.
*Faris, W H. Cicero, Hamilton co, Ind.
Fast, J J, Canton, Stark co, Ohio.
*Fastnacht,AG, Mt Holly Sprgs,Cumb'd co,Pa
Feddersen, A, Farina, Fayette co, Ills.
Fegely, H S, Lynnville, Lehigh co, Pa.
Fegely, H N, Mechanicsburg, Pa.
Feiertag, J, Aurora, Kane co, Ills.
Feistner, L, Febing, Nemaha co, Neb.
Feldman, A H, Canton, Stark co, Ohio.
*Felker, A C, Lewistown, Mifflin co, Pa.
*Felton, A C, Clarksville, Hunterdon co, NJ.
*Felts, P, Johnstown, Fulton co, N Y.
*Fenner, H K, Crestline, Crawford co, Ohio.
*Fenner, S. Upper Sandusky, Wyandot co, O.
*Fernsler, M, Millersburg, Dauphin co, Pa.
Fesperman, J H, Statesville, Iredell co, N C.
Fetzer, Chr'n A, Shannondale,Clarion co, Pa.
Feustel, G A, Effingham, Effingham co, Ills.
Fick, C J H, 286 Shawmut ave, Boston, Mass.
Fickeisen, J E, Lineville, Venango co, Pa.
Ficken, D M, Fort Madison, Lee co, Iowa.
*Fickinger, C, Bolivar, Tuscarawas co, Ohio.
Fikenscher, G, Versailles, Morgan co, Mo.
*Finckel, S G, Red Hook, Duchess co, N Y.
Finfrock, Aaron, Womelsdorf, Berks co, Pa.
Fink, J S, Harrison City, Westmorel'd co,Pa.
*Fink, R A, D D, Johnstown, Cambria co, Pa.
*Finkbiner, J W, Middletown, Dauphin co,Pa
*Firey, Milton J, Emporia, Lyon co, Kansas.
Fischer, A F H, Carver, Carver co, Minna.
*Fischer, G M, Rantoul, Livingston co, Ind.
Fischer, H, Seymour, Jackson co, Ind.
Fischer, H C, Port Chester, Westch'ter co,NY
Fishburn, J N, Maple, York co, Ont.
*Fisher, W E, Gettysburg, Adams co, Pa.
Fisher, W L, Milan, Ripley co. Ind.
*Fismer, A, Lanesville, La Salle co, Ind.
Fjeld, J N, Black Earth, Dane co, Wis.
Flachsbart, H, Pilot Knob, Iron co, Mo.
Flath, J F, East New York, Kings co, N Y.
*Fleck, H R, Mechanicsb'g, Cumberl'd co, Pa.
Fleckenstein, E J, Alexandria, Va.
Fleenor, Jas, Bristol, Sullivan co, Tenn.
Fleischmann, P, Kendallville, Noble co, Ind.
*Fleming, J W, Huntertown, Allen co, Ind.
*Fletcher, R H, Lock Haven, Clinton co, Pa.
Floren, S L, Muskegon, Mich.
*Focht, Jos R, McConnellsb'g, Fulton co, Pa.
Foehlinger, F W, Yorkville. N Y.
Foelsch, B, Cedar Falls, Bl'k Hawk co, Iowa.
*Foglesong, N P, Millersburg, Holmes co, O.
*Ford, Leander, Sharon, Walworth co, Wis.
Forsander, N, Sagetown, Henderson co, Ills.
*Forthman, Jno. Carlisle, Cumberland co, Pa.
*Foulk, D Z, Gettysburg, Adams co, Pa.
*Foust, D I, Shelby, Richland co, Ohio.
Foust, G D, Philadelphia, Pa.
Fox, A J, M D, Newton, Catawba co, N C.
Fox, J B, Emlenton, Venango co, Pa.
Fox, L A, Waynesboro', Augusta co, Va.
Fox, M L, Sandy Creek, Randolph co, N C.
Fox, W B, Sumneytown, Montgomery co, Pa.
Francis, S A K, 1431 S 10 st, Philadelphia, Pa.
Franke, F W, Delhi, Norfolk co, Ont.
Frank, C A, New Orleans, La.

Francke, A G G, Addison, Du Page co, Ills.
*Frazier, Jer'h, Blain, Perry Co, Pa.
Frederick, G W, 117 N 6 st, Philadelphia, Pa.
Frederking, C W R, Beecher, Will co, Ills.
Freese, H, New Auburn, Sibley co, Minn.
Frehner J, Arneckville, De Witt co, Texas.
Fremling, J, Stockholm, Pepin co, Wis.
Frese, A W, West Point, Cuming co, Neb.
Frese, E A, St Joseph, Mo.
Frese, E J, Logan, Dodge co, Neb.
Frese, J C L, Tonawanda, Erie co, N Y.
Frey, A E, Brooklyn, E D, N Y.
Frey, F L, New Boston, Winona co, Minn.
Frey, Wm A, Rockville, Tolland co, Conn.
Frich, J B, La Crosse, Wis.
Frich,W J L,Halfway Creek,La Crosse co,Wis.
*Frick, A C, Mt Morris, Ogle co, Ills.
Frick, W K, 2117 Bolton st, Philadelphia, Pa.
*Friday, J M, Harper's Ferry, Jef'n co,WVa.
Friedrich, G C. Washington,Washing'n co,Pa.
Friedrich W, Waconia, Carver co, Minna.
Friedrich,W J, Fall Creek, Eau Claire co,Wis.
Friedrichsen, A F, E Portl'd,Multnomah co,Or.
Frincke, C, 207 S Sharp st, Baltimore, Md.
Frincke,C J T, jun, Newtown, Long Is'd, N Y.
Fritschel, Prof G, Mendota, La Salle co, Ills.
Fritschel, Prof S, Mendota, La Salle co, Ills.
Fritz, John H, Shawnee, Monroe co, Pa.
Fritz, J, Martin's Ferry, Belmont co, Ohio.
Fritze, C A, Dayton, Ohio.
Fritze, J A, Monmouth, Adams co, Ind.
Frosch, W, ——, Texas.
Fruechtenicht, A, Ottawa, La Salle co, Ills.
Fry, Jacob, DD, Reading, Pa.
*Fryberger, S P, Malvern, Carroll co, Ohio.
Fuchs, A, Bath, Northampton co, Pa.
Fuehr, H, Berea, Cuyahoga co, Ohio.
Fuenfstueck,E A,Wilkesbarre,Luzerne co,Pa
Fuerbringer, O, Frankenmuth,Sag. co,Mich
*Fulmer, Jonas, Mendota, La Salle co, Ills.
*Funk, Isaac K, Pittsburg, Pa.

Gable, Z H, Reading, Berks co, Pa.
Gangnusz, H, Sebewaing, Huron co, Mich.
Gasz, J, Davenport, Scott co, Iowa.
Gartner, G F,Germantown, Philadelphia, Pa
Gaumer, G, Venango, Pa.
Gausewitz, C, Iron Ridge, Dodge co, Wis.
*Gaus, Henry, Portl'd, Multnomah co,Oregon.
Gebauer, C, Yelloway, Knox co, Ohio.
*Geiger, A M, Van Wert, Ohio.
Geiger, C, Oak Land, Colorado co, Texas.
*Geiger, Prof H R,DD,Springfield,Clark co,O.
*Geiger, J, Millville, Butler co, Ohio.
Gelmuyden, S, Milwaukee, Wis.
Geissenger, D H, Lancaster, Pa.
Geissenhainer,AT,1838 MtVernon st,Phila,Pa.
Geissenhainer, F W, DD, 106 E 14 st,N York.
*Gelwicks, C A, Elvira, Clinton co, Iowa
Gensike, T, Hortonville, Outagamie co,Wis.
Georgii, E C, Fowler, Clinton co, Mich.
Gerhardt, L, Leacock, Lancaster co, Pa.
Gerhardt,Wm,Martinsb'g, Berkeley co,W Va.
Gerken, G, Havana, Mason co, Ills.
Geskensmeier, J F, Venice, Erie co, Ohio.
Gerlach, M, Waverly, Iowa.
Germann, C A, Peru, Miami co, Ind.
Germann, P F, Cottonwood Falls, Kansas.
Gerndt, L H, 16 State st, New York, N Y.
Gerndt, C R, Webster, Monroe co. N Y.
Geschwind, L H, Lima, Allen co, Ohio.
Geszler, J, Fairbank, Buchanan co, Iowa.
Geyer, C A, Wellsville, Allegheny co, N Y.

Geyer, L, Carlinville, Macoupin co, Ills.
*Gheen, Peter, Shipman, Macoupin co, Ills.
Giese, Prof E F, Newark, Wayne co, N Y.
Giesecke, E, Davenport, Scott co, Iowa.
Giesz Henry, Jonestown, Lebanon co, Pa.
Gift, A E, Columbus, Ohio.
Gilbert, D M, Winchester, Shenandoah co,Va.
Gilbert, Prof H, Greenville, Mercer co, Pa.
*Gilbreath, J L, Vandalia. Fayette co. Ills.
*Gilbreath, W M, Salesville, Guernsey co, O.
Ginger, J, New Staunton, Westm'land co, Pa.
Gjaldaker, T B, Silver Lake, Worth co, Wis.
Gjertsen, J P, Stoughton, Dane co, Wis.
Gjertsen, M L, Leland, La Salle co, Ills.
*Gladhill, John T, Galt, Whiteside co, Ills.
Glenn, T A, Webster. Winston co, Miss.
Gloor, F, Galveston, Texas.
Goebel, J, Bryan, Williams co, Ohio.
Gochling, C, Brooklyn, N Y.
Goehringer, J G, Mascoutah. St Clair co, Ills.
Goeszling, F, MD, Troy, N Y.
*Goethe, Matthias, Sacramento, Cal.
*Goettman, J G, Alleghany city, Pa.
Goetz, J, Ellenville, Ulster co, N Y.
Goldammer, C F, Green Bay, Wis.
Gomph, Geo. Pittsford, Monroe co, N Y.
*Goodlin, J Y, York, York co, Pa.
Goodman, H, Statesville, Iredell co, N C.
Goszweiler, J, San Antonia, Texas.
Gottleib, F E, Port Richmond, Staten Is, NY
Gotsch, G M, Ph D, Men.phis, Tenn.
Gotsch, G T, Lombard, Du Page co, Ills.
*Gotwald, L A, DD, York, York co, Pa.
*Gotwald, Wm H, Milton, Northumb'd co,Pa
Grabau, J, Buffalo, N Y.
Grabau, Prof J A A, Buffalo, N Y.
Grabau, Wm, Cedarsburg, Ozaukee co, Wis.
*Grabill, J M, Everett, Bedford co, Pa.
Graeber, C A, Meriden, New Haven co, Conn.
Graebner, J H P, St Charles, Mo.
Graef, D, Dashwood, Huron co, Ont.
Graef, P, Augusta, St Charles co, Mo.
*Graef, Philip, Washington, D C.
Graef, W, Brenham, Washington co, Texas.
Graepp, C A, Pembroke, Renfrew co, Ont.
Graepp, L W, Neustadt, Ont.
Graeszle, J, Bucyrus, Crawford co, Ohio.
Graetz, F A, Columbus, Ohio.
Graetz, R, Blackswamp, Sandusky co, Ohio.
Graetzel, H. Cube Hill, Baltimore co, Md.
Grahn, H, 1009 S 4th st, Philadelphia, Pa.
Gram, C, Milwaukee, Wis.
Gram, J, East Boston, Mass.
Granere, Prof C O, Paxton, Ford co, Ills.
Grau, W, ——, Mo.
Graul, J, Burton, Washington co, Texas.
Graven, G L, Vermillion, Dakota.
*Graves, U, 1836 Monument st, Balto, Md.
Green, L E, Madelia, Watonwan co, Minna.
Greenwald, E, DD, Lancaster, Pa.
Greever, J B, Rural Retreat, Wythe co, Va.
Greever, J J,Burke's Garden, Tazew'l co.Va.
*Gregory, H L, Yuba City. Sutter co, Cal.
Greif, A D, Serbin, Lee co, Texas.
Greiner, Prof J B, Marion, Smythe co, Va.
*Griffith, J G, Clermont, Columbia co. N Y.
Groening, J, Marine City, St Clair co, Mich.
*Groenmiller, J G, Falls City, Rich'n co, Neb.
Groetheim, J, Ft Howard, Brown co, Wis.
Groff, J R, Easton, Northampton co, Pa.
Groh, L, Boyertown, Berks co, Pa.
*Groseclose, L C, Irving, Montgomery co, Ills.
Grosz, Charles, Buffalo, N Y.

Grossberger, A C, Buffalo, N Y.
*Grosscup, D P, Iowa City, Johnson co, Iowa.
Grosze, F M, Oak Park, Cook co, Ills.
Grosze, T J, Chicago, Ills.
*Grossman, H C, Tremont, Schuylkill co, Pa.
Groszmann, G, Prof St Sebald, Clayton co, Iowa
Groth, F, Dayton, Montgomery co, Ohio.
Grothe, E A, Lock Haven, Clinton co, Pa.
Gruber, G, Van Wert, Ohio.
Gruber, K T, Seward, Seward co, Nebraska.
Gruhler, J, Shenand'h City, Schuylkill co, Pa
Grunert, J, Liverpool, Medina co, Ohio.
Grupe, H F, Cape Girardeau, Mo.
Grupe, H F, C C, Champaign, Ills.
*Guard, J L, Camden, Carroll co, Ind.
Guemmer, H, Lawrenceb'g, Dearborn co, Ind.
Guensch, G F W, Minersville, Schuylkill co, Pa
Guenther, F, Burr Oak, La Crosse co, Wis.
Guenther, J P, Geneseo, Henry co, Ills.
Guenther, Prof M, St Louis, Mo.
Guldbrandsen, G, Gayville, Yankton co, Dak.
*Gulick, W W, Germantown, Columbia co, N Y.
Gunnersen, Prof S, Minneapolis, Minn.
Guntrum, E, Chicago, Ills.
*Gurtefson, J M, Verona, Lawrence co, Mo.
Gyr, H, St Ansgar, Mitchell co, Iowa.

Haack, H J, Hortonville, Outagamie co, Wis.
Haar, G, Den'son, Crawford co, Iowa.
Haas, J, Owosso, Shiawassee co, Mich.
Haase, J, Appleton, Outagamie co, Wis.
Hackenberger, F A W, Lincoln, Neb.
*Hackenberg, J A, Ashland, Schuylkill co, Pa
Hacker, J, Pocahontas, Cape Girardeau co, Mo.
Hackhousen, H, Sand Creek, Dunn co, Wis.
Haeger, J D, Pittsfield, Berkshire co, Mass.
Haese, H, Newville, Vernon co, Wis.
Haessler, T, Crete, Saline co, Neb.
Hagedorn, H W, Neenah, Winnebago co, Wis.
Hagestad, O J K, Martell, Pierce co, Wis.
Hagen, A O, St James, Watonwanco co, Minn.
Hahn, A A, Upper Tract, Pendleton co, W Va.
Hahn, J L, Sebervain, Huron co, Mich.
Hahn, J G, Roseville, Macomb co, Mich.
Hahn, J M, Staunton, Macoupin co, Ills.
Hahn, T F, ——,
*Haithcox, H C, Muncy, Lycoming co, Pa.
Hakinson, C W, Randolph, Riley co, Kansas.
Halboth, M, Boeuf Creek, Franklin co, Mo.
*Halderman, G W, Lancaster, Fairfield co, O.
Halfman, L, Yorkville, New York city, N Y.
*Hall, H H, Monongahela City, Pa.
*Hall, John, Woodview, Morrow co, Ohio.
Halland, B M, Stanton, Montgomery co, Iowa.
Hallman, J P, Fort Motte, Orange co, S C.
Hallerberg, W, Quincy, Adams co, Ills.
Halvorsen, H, Fort Ridgely, Renv'e co, Minn.
Halvorson, J, Fort Ridgely, Minn'a.
*Hamilton, Dr J, Butler, Montgomery co, Ills.
*Hamma, M W, Springfield, Clark co, Ohio.
*Hammer, G, Van Wert, Ohio.
*Hammond, J L, Shuey's Mills, Wis.
Hancher, J K, Millpoint, Sullivan co, Tenn.
Hande, H, Estherville, Emmett co, Iowa.
Hannawald, L, Plattsmouth, Cass co, Neb.
Hansen, O, St Ansgar, Mitchell co, Iowa.
Hanser, O, Aspelund, Goodhue co, Minna.
Hanser, W G H, Baltimore, Md.
Hanser, C J O, Fort Wayne, Ind.
Hantz, Jac M, Monongahela City, Pa.
*Harbaugh, D, Waterville, Marshall co, Kan.
Harkey, Jas M, Claremont, Richland co, Ills.
*Harkey, Jas S, Valatie, Columbia co, N Y.

Harkey, S L, Mt Pleasant, Westmor'd co, Pa.
*Harkey, S W, DD, Washing'n, Tazewell co, Ill.
Harmening, H, Dissen, Cape Girardeau co, Mo.
*Harpel, M, Reading, Pa.
*Harpster, J H, Miss'y, Guntur, India.
*Harrington, S P, Abilene, Dickinson co, Kan.
*Harris, J G, Bellefontaine, Logan co, Ohio.
*Harrison, Prof P L, Gettysb'g, Adams co, Pa.
Harry, J H, Concord, N C.
Harstad, B A, Goose River, Minn'a.
Harter, G, Amanda, Fairfield co, Ohio.
Harter, G A, Auburn, De Kalb co, Ind.
*Hartman, A S, 174 Dean st, Brooklyn, N Y.
Hartmann, C F, ——, Matteson co, Ills.
*Hartsock, A J, Boalsburg, Centre co, Pa.
Hartwig, A, ——, Mo.
Haskarl, Dr W R C, 2241 N 2d, st, Phila, Pa.
Hasselquist, Prof T N, DD, Paxton, Ford co, Ills
Hassler, J W, New Holland, Lancaster co, Pa.
Hassler, T, Olive Branch, Lancaster co, Neb.
Hatz, F W, La Crosse, Wis.
Hatlestad, O J, Milwaukee, Wis.
Hittstaedt, W. Monroe, Monroe co, Mich.
*Hauer, D J, DD, Hanover, York co, Pa.
*Hauer, W C, Tarlton, Pickaway co, Ohio.
Hauser, J, Cottage Grove, Dane co, Wis.
Hauszmann, C F, Brooklyn, N Y.
Hawkins, Jac, Shepherdsl'n, Jefferson co, W Va
*Hawkins, W W, Salem, Franklin co, Tenn.
*Hawkinson, C, Randolph, Riley co, Kansas.
*Hay, Prof Chas A, DD, Gettysb'g, Adams co, Pa
*Heck, J H, Schoharie, N Y.
Hecke, W, New Haven, Macomb co, Mich.
Heckel, J, Knoxville, Knox co, Tenn.
Hedeen, Erick, N London, Randolph co, Minn.
Hedengran, C A, Chisago Lake, Minna.
Hedenschoug, A W, Chicago, Ills.
*Hedges, S A, York Springs, Adams co, Pa.
Heiberg, J A, 276 First st, Chicago, Ills.
Heid, P, Peoria, Ills.
*Heigerd, H'y, Effingham, Atchison co, Kan.
*Height, A R, Perryville, Perry co, Mo.
Heilig, Theo, Riegelsville, Bucks co, Pa.
*Heilig, W M, Lutherville, Baltimore co, Md.
*Heilig, J S, James' Creek, Hunting'n co, Pa.
*Heilman, L M, Harrisburg, Pa.
Heimenthal, —, Kilbourn Road, Miles co, Wis.
Heinemann, W, Worden, Madison co, Ills.
Heiniger, John, Hannibal, Marion co, Mo.
Heinrichs, H B, Watertown, Jefferson co, Wis.
Heintz, G C, Crown Point, Ind.
*Heisler, W L, Mifflinburg, Union co, Pa.
*Heisler, M L, Hughesville, Lycoming co, Pa.
Heitmuller, A, Columbus, Bartholomew co, Ind.
Helsem, C J, West Eau Claire, Wis.
Helbig, R, Boscobel, Grant co, Wis.
Held, A H M, 198 Allen st, New York city.
Helland, K, Wiota, Lafayette co, Wis.
Helle, W F, Upper Sandusky, Ohio.
Hellestvedt, J A, Fargo, Dakota Territory.
*Helsell, Jesse, Clarence, Cedar co, Iowa.
*Helwig, A, Brookville, Montg'y co, Ohio.
*Helwig, Prof J B, Springfield, Clark co, O.
Hemborg, C A, W Dayton, Webster co, Iowa.
*Heming, J W, Huntertown, Allen co, Ind.
Hempeler, J H, Helena, Johnson co, Neb.
Hempeler, J G, Metropolis, Massac co, Ills.
*Hemperly, G W, Sunbury, North'd co, Pa.
Henagan, A S, Salis, Attala co, Miss.
Henckell, E, Washington, D C.
*Henderson, J W, Lanark, Carroll co, Ills.
Hengerer, J A, Blossom, Erie co, N Y.
Hengist, H T, Brookfield, Trumbull co, Ohio.

Henke, Wm, Aurora, Kane co, Ills.
Henkel, A, Burr Oak, St Joseph co, Mich.
Henkel, D M, Mt Pleasant, Cabarrus co, N C.
Henkel, E S, Waynetown, Montg'y co, Ind.
Henkel, H, Logan, Hocking co, Ohio.
Henkel, P C, Gravelton, Wayne co, Mo.
Henkel, Socrates, N Market, Shenand'h co,Va.
Hennicke, F T, Weissport, Carbon co, Pa.
*Hennicke, Ch, New York city.
*Hennicke, H, Roseville, Macomb co, Mich.
*Hennighausen, F P, 143 Sharp st, Balto, Md
*Henry, S, Phillipsburg, Warren co, N J.
*Henry, E S, Pine Grove, Schuylkill co, Pa.
Henry, Sam S, Hinkletown, Lancast'r co, Pa.
Hentz, J P, Germantown, Montgomery co, O.
Herbst, Richard, Columbus, Ohio.
Herbst, K E, Sheldon, Allen co, Ind.
Hering, Wm M, Lima, Allen co, Ohio.
Her, J, Cohocton, Steuben co, N Y.
Herrmann, C F, State Centre, Iowa.
*Herring, S E, Duncannon, Perry co, Pa.
Herschmann, L, Boscobel, Grant co, Iowa.
Hershiser, J F, Tippecanoe City, Miami co, O.
Hertel, W, Highland Centre, Wapello co. Iowa.
Hertrich, S, Wells, Faribault co, Minn.
Hertwig, A, Leaf Valley, Douglass co, Minn.
Herzberger, F A,7218th st, Pittsb'g, S side,Pa.
Herzer, J A, Minneapolis, Minna.
*Hesson, A J, Mercersburg, Franklin co, Pa.
*Heydenreich, Prof L W, 30 N Wm st, N Y.
Heydler, E, Rochester, N Y.
Heyer, M, Ashf'd Hollow, Cattaraugus co,NY
Hieber, E, Matteson, Cook co, Ills.
Hieber, J M, Edgerton, Williams co, Ohio.
Hieberg, J A, Chicago, Ills.
Hild, J G H, Mishawaka, St Joseph co, Ind.
Hilgendorf, J, Omaha, Nebraska.
Hill, R, Allentown, Pa.
Hill, R O, Creston, Ogle co, Ills.
Hillemann, H, Wilson, Winona co, Minn.
Hillemann, J G M, Altamont, Effing'm co, Ill.
*Hiller, Alfred, German Valley, Morris co,N J.
Hiller, C G, Pomeroy, Meigs co, Ohio.
Hillpot, J, Richland Centre, Bucks co, Pa.
*Hills, B F, North Liberty, Johnson co, Iowa.
Hilpert, F, Kohlsville, Washington co, Wis.
Himmler, J C, Humberstone,Welland co, Ont.
*Hinderer, J, Troy, Miami co, Ohio.
Hinnenthal, C, Milwaukee co, Wis.
Hinterleitner,G A,Pottsville,Schuylkill co,Pa.
Hippee, L, North Williamsb'g, Dundee co,Ont
Hirschmann, J L, Chattanooga, Tenn.
Hjort, O J, Dahlby, Alamakee co, Iowa.
Hobstad, O E, Canton, Dakotah.
Hocanzon, L A, Waseca, Waseca co, Minna.
Hochstetter, C W, Indianapolis, Ind.
Hockman, M H, Carrollton, Carroll co, Ohio.
Hodtwalker, A, Bayview, Milwaukee co, Wis.
Hoeck, R, Poughkeepsie, Duchess co, N Y.
Hoelsche, J, Waterloo, Province co, Ont.
Hoelter, L, Quincy, Ills.
Hoelzel, G, Ripon, Fond du Lac co, Wis.
Hoemann, H W, Colfax, Tremont co, Col.
Hoenecke, A, Milwaukee, Wis.
Hoernicke, G H, Sheboygan, Wis.
Hoerr, J, Baltimore, Md.
Hoffman, E, Albany, N Y.
Hoffman, J J, Sheboygan Falls, Wis.
Hoffman, J O, St Paris, Champaign co, Ohio.
Hoffman, J U, Canajoharie, Montg'y co, N Y.
Hoffmann, A, West Newton, Nicollet co, Minn.
Hoffmann, H, W Granville, Milwaukee co,Wis.
Hofstad, O E, Canton, Lincoln co, Dak'a.

Hoñus, A, Columbus, Calorado co, Texas.
Hogboe, B, Ashland, Dodge co, Minna.
Hokanson, M F, Munterv'e,Wapello co, Iowa.
Holland, Prof G W, Walhalla, S C.
Holland, R C, Madison C II, Va.
Hollman, —, Orangeburg, S C.
*Holloway, II C, Cumb'd, Alleghany co, Md.
Holls, F Wm, Millstadt, St Clair co, Ills.
Holls, C G, Mt Vernon, Westchester co, N Y.
Holm, H G, Buena Vista, Tuscar's co, Ohio.
*Holman, S A, 528 N 38th st, Philad'a, Pa.
Holmgren, Anders V, Keokuk, Iowa.
Holseth, M C, Estherville, Emmet co, Iowa.
Holst, C, Troy, Madison co, Ills.
Holterman, H H, Effingham, Ills.
Holterman, P H, Kimmswick, Jeff'n co, Mo.
*Holtgreve, II H, Staunton. Macoupin co, Ills
*Holtkamp, H H, Clayton, Adams co, Ills.
Homme, E J, Winchester, Winnebago co,Wis.
*Honeycutt,J E, Upper Strasb'g, Franklin,Pa.
Honour, J H, Charleston, S C.
Hoppe, C F W, Rochester, N Y.
Hoppe, A F, New Orleans, La.
*Hooper, P S, Columbus Grove, Putnam co,O
Hoops, H, Bandyne Station, Wis.
*Hoover, F T. Leechburg, Armstrong co, Pa.
Hordorf, A, Sandusky City, Ohio.
Horine, M C. Danville, Montour co, Pa.
Horn, E T, Chestnut Hill, Philadelphia, Pa.
Horn, F, Geneseo, Henry co. Ills.
Horn, G, Robin, Benton co. Iowa.
Horn, J, Mt Hope, Holmes co, Ohio.
Hornberger, J F, Wine Hill, Randolph co, Ills.
Horne, A R, Prof, Kutztown, Berks co, Pa.
Horst, John, Red Wing, Goodhue co, Minna.
Horst, H, Hilliard, Franklin co, Ohio.
Hosius, A, Columbus, Colorado co, Texas.
Hough, G A, Orangeburg, S C.
House, A B, Rochester, Fulton co, Ind.
*Houseman, J H, Ginger Hill, Wash'n co,Pa.
Houser, Joseph, Midway, Greene co, Tenn.
Hovde, B, New Lisbon, Juneau co, Wis.
*Howbert, A R, Bellefontaine, Crawford co,O.
Hoyer, J A, Princeton, Greenlake co, Wis.
Hub, J G, Minneapolis, Minna.
*Huber, Eli, Nebraska City, Nebraska Ter'y.
*Huber, J J, Fairview, Cedar co, Iowa.
Huber E, Mason, Mason co, Texas.
Hubbert,Prof W E, Mt Pleas't,Cabarrus co, NC
Hudtloff, W, Wausau, Marathon co, Wis.
Huegli, J A, Detroit, Mich.
Hufford, R W, Cincinnati, Ohio.
Hugo, C F, W Bremen, Marshall co, Ind.
*Hull, Wm, Hudson, Columbia co, N Y.
Hult, A, Campello, Plymouth co, Mass.
Hultgren, C O, Jamest'n, Chaut'qua co, N Y.
Humbert, David K, Lyons, Berks co, Pa.
Humberger, J, Canal Fulton, Stark co, Ohio.
Hunt, B H, 4111 Hutton st, W Philadel'a, Pa.
Hunton, J H, Bridgewater, Nova Scotia.
Hunziker, J J, Herzhorn, Renville co, Minna.
Hunziker, H, Biehle, Perry co, Mo.
Hunziker, S, Cardington, Morrow co, Ohio.
Huntzinger, F K, Reading, Pa.
Hursh, I, Versailles, Dark co, Ohio.
Husman, W F, East Cleveland, Ohio.
Hvid, P J, Silverlake, North co, Iowa.
Hvistendahl, C, San Francisco, Cal.
*Hyman, S B, Jeffersontown, Jefferson co, Ky

Ide, C, Iowa City, Iowa.
*Ide, Er, Laurel, Pr George's co, Md.
*Imhoff, A J, Leipsic, Putnam co. Ohio.

Isenschmidt, Paul, Wilmington, Del.
Isensee, J F, Weisberg, Dearborn co, Ind.
Iske, F, Ida, Monroe co, Mich.
Iversen, N W, Chicago, Ills.

Jaastad, E, Rushford, Fillmore co, Minn.
Jackson, And, Bevens Cr'k, Carver co, Minn.
Jacobs, Prof H E, Gettysburg, Adams co, Pa.
Jacobsen, A, Perry, Dane co, Wis.
Jacobsen, C B, 216 Franklin st, Philad'a. Pa.
Jacobsen, J C, Decorah, Winnesh'k co, Minn.
Jacobson, Jac D, Decorah, Winnesh'k co, Iowa
Jaebker, G H, Po P O, Allen co, Ind.
Jaekel, C, New Castle, Lawrence co, Pa.
Jaekel, Th, Milwaukee, Wis.
Jaeger, C, Two Rivers, Manitowoc co, Wis.
Jaeger, C M, Reading, Berks co, Pa.
Jaeger, Gottleib F J, Kleinsville, Berks co, Pa.
Jaeger, Joshua, Allentown, Lehigh co, Pa.
Jaeger, T H, Patricksburg, Owen co, Ind.
Jaeger, Th J, Patricksburg, Owen co, Ind.
Jaeger, Thos T, Reading, Berks co, Pa.
Jaeggli, R, Fayetteville, Fayette co, Texas.
Jahn, J, Brownsville, Houston co, Minn.
James, B H, 216 Franklin st, Philad'a, Pa.
Janzow, C L, Leavenworth, Kansas.
Jelden, T, Toronto, Ontario.
*Jenkins, Wm, Shelbyville, Bedford co, Tenn.
Jensen, Erek, Mound Springs, Jackson co,Wis
Jensen, C P, Indianapolis, Ind.
Jesse, F, Giddings, Washington co, Texas.
Joerlander, E N, Sweden.
Johannes, J M, Pekin, Tazewell co, Ills.
Johannesen, E, Story City, Iowa.
Johansson, C F, 450 Shawmut av, Bost'n,Mass
Johl, F W S, Claremont, Dodge co, Minn.
John, F W, Tecumseh, Johnson co, Nebraska.
Johnson, A, West Eau Claire, Wis.
Johnson, J, Paxton, Ford co, Ills.
Johnson, P L, Rio, Columbia co, Wis.
Johnson, Th, Norseland, Nicollet co, Minn.
*Johnston, E S, Emmittsburg, Fred'k co, Md.
Jonas, E, Ahnapee, Kewaunee co, Wis.
*Jones, L S, Bridgeville, Muskingum co, O.
Jones, E H, Gravel Springs, Fred'k co, Va.
Jordan, G, Castroville, Medina co, Texas.
Jox, J H, Logansport, Ind.
Juengel, R, Jonesville, Bartholomew co, Ind.
Juersen, F, Chicago, Ills.
Jukam, O G, Calmus, Clinton co, Iowa.
*Julian, W A, Mill Hill, Cabarrus co, N C.
Jungck, F J T, Jackson,Cape Girardeau co,Mo.
Jungk, Carl, Ridgeway, Winneshiek co, Iowa.
Junker, L E, Morrison, Brown co, Wis
Juul, S O, New York city.
Juve, T O, Rising Sun, Crawford co, Wis.

Kaeding, Chrs F, Perrysburg, Wood co, O.
Kaehler, E W, Lancaster, Fairfield co, Ohio.
Kaehler, F A, Germantown, Philad'a, Pa.
Kaehler, F C C, Saugerties, Ulster co, N Y.
Kaehler, H C, Rome, N Y.
*Kaempfer, J, Sr, Glen Rock, York co, Pa.
Kaeselitz, A, Marquette, Mich.
*Kaessmann, C F A, St Joseph, Mo.
*Kahrs, H., Winesburg, Holmes co, O.
*Kain, D F, Monmouth, Adams co, Ind.
*Kallstroem, P J, 664 Baltie st, Brooklyn, N Y.
Kanold, H, Walcottsville, Niagara co, N Y.
Kanning, F W, Denver, Bremer co, Iowa.
Karrar, P, Maple Station, Allen co, Ind.
Karrer, J, Hadley, La Pere co, Mich.
Karth, F, Independence, Montgom'y co, Kan.

Kaselitz, C H O, Brooklyn, E D, N Y.
Kasa, O. J, Fergus Falls, Minn.
Kaspar, J, High Hill, Texas.
*Kast, A J B, Mechanicsburg, Cumb'd co, Pa.
Katt, H, Stacey's, Vanderburgh co, Ind.
Katthain, J G O, Hoyleton, Wash'ton co, Ills.
*Kauffman, J C, Springfield, Clark co, Ohio.
*Keedy, C L, M D, Waynesboro', Fr'klin co, Pa.
*Keefer, R, Wooster, Ohio.
*Keil, W G, Senecaville, Guernsey co, Ohio.
*Kekler, W, Waynesboro', Franklin co, Pa.
Keller, C F, Thiensville, Ozaukee co, Wis.
*Keller, Henry, Cobleskill, Schoh. co, N Y.
*Keller, Jacob, Corydon, Harrison co, Ind.
*Keller, J B, Williamsport, Wash'n co, Md.
*Keller, L, Funkstown, Washington co, Md.
*Keller, W H, Corunna, De Kalb co, Ind.
*Kelso, S, Walton, Cass co, Ind.
Kemerer, D M, Saegerstown, Crawford co, Pa.
Kemmer, B E, Rokeby, Morgan co, Ohio.
Kenter, A, Charlestown, Redwood co, Minn.
*Keplinger, E J, Grasshopper Falls, Kansas.
*Kepner, D K, Slatington, Lehigh co, Pa.
Kern, J J, Hebron, Jefferson co, Nebraska.
*Kerr, J J, Myersville, Frederick co, Md.
Kessler, C, Logansville, Sauk co, Wis.
Ketchie, W R, China Grove, Rowan co, N C.
*Ketterman, W H, Jefferson, Pa.
Keyl, S, New York city, N Y.
*Kieffer, S P, Reedsburg, Wayne co, Ohio.
Kilian, J, Serbin, Lee co, Texas.
Kilian, J, Theresa, Dodge co, Wis.
Kimball, W, China Grove, Rowan co, N C.
Kindborg, J W, Titusville, Crawford co, Pa.
*King, John, Athens, Limestone co, Ala.
*King, R. J, Shelbyville, Bedford co, Tenn.
Kirkeberg, O L, Indianapolis, Ind.
*Kirtland, A B, Nevada, Wyandot co Ohio.
Kiser, J F, Fincastle, Va.
Kissel, A J, Sulphur Springs, Crawford co, O.
*Kistler, J, Tyrone, Blair co, Pa.
Kistler, R B, Cherryville, Northamp'n co, Pa.
*Kitch, John W, Marysville, Marion co, Iowa.
Kittel, G C C, Carrick, Alleghany co, Pa.
Kitzmiller, J H A, Freeport, Armst'g co, Pa.
Klein, S S, Ringtown, Schuylkill co, Pa.
Kleinert, F A, Dotyville, Wis.
Kleinhans, P, Howard's Gr'e, Shebo'n co,Wis.
Kleinlein, P, Keokuk Junction, Adams co,Ills.
Kleist, F, Washington, Franklin co, Mo.
Kleppisch, C S, Belleville, St Clair co, Ills.
Klindworth, Prof J, Galena, Jo Daviess co,Ills.
Klindworth, P,Wm Penn,Washington co, Tex.
*Kline, D, Clarksville, Hunterdon co, N J.
*Klinefelter, F, Greencastle, Franklin co, Pa.
*Kling, J, East Schodack, Renss'r co, N Y.
*Kling, Marcus, Lawyersville, Schoh co,N Y.
Klingman, S T, Ann Arbor, Mich.
*Klock, Nellis, Knox, Albany co, N Y.
Klockmeyer, H, Lincoln, Neb.
*Kloss, Daniel, Lykens, Dauphin co, Pa.
Kluge, A, Reedsville, Manitowoc co. Wis.
Knapp, C L, Lancaster, Erie co, N Y.
Knappe, C, ———
Knauth, E, Cardington, Morrow co, Ohio.
Knechle, G, Milwaukee, Mich.
Knief, L E, Marysville, Union co, Ohio.
Knisely, U J, Newcomerst'n,Tuscarawas co,O.
*Knodle, Hiram, Mercersb'g, Franklin co, Pa.
Knoll, R, Beardstown, Cass co, Ills.
Knuth, K W, Sugar Grove, Fairfield co,Ohio.
Koch, C, Fredericksburg, Gillespie co, Texas.
Koch, H, Grand Rapids, Kent co, Mich.

Koch, V, Versailles, Dark co, Ohio.
Koeberle, Th, Atlanta, Fulton co, Ga.
Koeberlin, K, Greenville, Dark co, Ohio.
Koehler, J, Fountain City, Buffalo co, Wis.
Koehler, Philip, Hustisford, Dodge co, Wis.
Koehler, R, Union Hill, Kankakee co, Ills.
Koenig, F, New York City.
Koenig, II, Evansville, Vanderburgh co, Ind.
Koenig, L, Yonkers, Westchester co, N Y.
Koepplin, J M, Olean, Ripley co, Ind.
Koerner, C, St Louis, Mo.
Koerner, C, Pottstown, Montgomery co, Pa.
Koerner, C J. Whitewater, Walworth co,Wis.
Koerner, F T, 367 Grand st, Brooklyn, N Y.
Koerner, K, Random Park, Sheboygan co,Wis.
Koestering, J F, Altenburg, Perry co, Mo.
Kogler, J, Minneapolis, Minn.
Kohler, J, Stroudsburg, Monroe co, Pa.
Kohler, S, Rochester, N Y.
*Koller, J C, Glen Rock, York co, Pa.
Kolbe, O, Martinsville, Niagara co, N Y.
Kolbe, F H, Green Isle, Sibley co, Minn.
Kollmorgen, C, Carmi, White co, Ills.
Koons, Prof Ed J, Jonestown, Lebanon co,Pa.
Koren, V, Decorah, Winneshiek co, Iowa.
Kornbaum, E, Sr, Baden Baden, Bond co, Ill.
Kornbaum, E, Jr, Pemberville, Wood co, O.
*Koser, D, Addison, Somerset co, Pa.
*Koser, J A, Gettysburg, Pa.
Kothe, D, Mount Olive, Macoupin co, Ills.
*Krack, J, Dongola, Union co, Ills.
Krafft, H A, Archibald, Fulton co, Ohio.
Kraemer, D A, Iowa City, Iowa.
Kramer, K W, Boston, Mass.
Kramer, W, Zilwaukee, Saginaw co, Mich.
Kramlich, B E, Kutztown, Berks co, Pa.
Kramlich, M J, Nazareth, North'ton co, Pa.
Kranz, J G, New Hamburg, Mercer co, Pa.
Krapf, W, Victoria, Victoria co, Texas.
Krause, L F E, Lobethal, South Australia.
Krauss, E A W, Cedarburg, Ozauk co, Wis.
Krauth, Prof C P, D D, L L D, 4004 Pine st,
   Philadelphia, Pa.
Krebs, L, Mansfield, Richland co, Ohio.
Krebs, K G, Swan Creek, Mich.
Krebs, W, Tonica, La Salle co, Ills.
*Krechting, J P, Amsterdam, Montg co,NY.
Kreps, B, Midway, Barnwell co, S C.
Kretzsmar, E W, Prairie du Chien, Wis.
Kretzschmar, H, Bear Lake, Freeb'n co, Minn
Kretzmann, C, Cape Girardeau, Mo.
Kreuter, H M, Harrison, Hamilton co, Ohio.
Kribbs, J A, Kittanning, Armstrong co, Pa.
Krog, II J G, Menomonee, Dunn co, Wis.
Krognaess, S M, Chicago, Ills.
Kroenke, F J, Riga, Lenawee co, Mich.
Kronberg, S J, Evansville, Douglass co,Minn.
Krohn, J, Chicago, Ills.
Krotel, G F, DD, 49 W 21 st, New York City.
Krug, P, Newark, N J.
Krumsieg, T G A, Henderson, Sibley co,Minn.
Kucher, J, Ft Wayne, Ind.
Kuchler, M, Greenville, Mercer co, Pa.
Kuechle, G, Milwaukee, Wis.
Kuegele, F, Cumberland, Alleghany co, Md.
Kuehn, C, 206 E 105 st, New York City.
Kuehn, II, Indianapolis, Ind.
Kuehne, A, Stapleton, Staten Island, N Y.
Kuendig, John J, Reading, Pa.
Kuempflein, G, ——, Iowa.
*Kuhl, Conrad, Carthage, Hancock co, Ills.
*Kuhlman, J F, Ponca, Dixon co, Neb.

Kuhn, A, Mankato, Blue Earth co, Minn.
*Kuhn, D A, Nevada, Wyandotte co, Ohio.
*Kuhn, Francis, Western, Linn co, Iowa.
Kuhn, II B, Port Jervis, Orange co, N Y.
*Kuhns, II W, Newberry, S C.
*Kuhns, L M, Canton, Stark co, Ohio.
Kunkelman, J A, 1314 Spring G st, Phila, Pa.
Kunkelman, M L, Zelienople, Butler co, Pa.
Kuntz, D, Nazareth, Northampton co, Pa.
Kuntz, J J, Mulberry, Clinton co, Ind.
Kuntz, W H, Schuylkill Haven, Sch'll co, Pa.
Kunz, J G, Julietta, Marion co, Ind.
*Kurtz, Adolph, ——, Md.
Kurz, A, (Bel-Air road,) Baltimore, Md.
Kusz, A C, Town Line, Erie co, N Y.
*Kutz, H D, Harrisburg, Pa.
Kyser, D, Lexington, S C.

*Lacker, Ph, Salamonia, Jay co, Ind.
Lagerman, F, Paxton, Ford co, Ill.
Lagerstroem, J G, St Peter, Nicollet co, Minn.
Laird, Samuel, Pittsburgh, Pa.
Laitzle, W G, Catawissa, Columbia co, Pa.
*Lake, J W, New Chester, Adams co, Pa.
Landgraf, G, Decatur, Macon co, Ills.
Landgrebe, G, St Ansgar, Mitchell co, Iowa.
Landmark, Prof O, Decorah,Winne'k co, Iowa.
*Lane, P P, Hampstead, Carroll co, Md.
Lang, II, Fremont, Sandusky co, Ohio.
*Lang, J M, E Germantown, Wayne co, Ind.
*Lang, W W, Mt Vernon, Knox co, Ohio.
Lange, A, Watertown, Jefferson co,Wis.
*Lange, B. ——
Lange, C II R, Chicago, Ills.
Lange, F W, Gooch's Mills, Cooper co, Mo.
Lange, P, Menomonee, Dunn co, Wis.
Lange, W J B, Valparaiso, Porter co, Ind.
*Lape, T, Athens, Green co, N Y.
Larsen, P F L,Decorah,Winneskiek co, Iowa.
Larsen, T, Harmony, Fillmore, Minn.
Larsen, S G, Ithaca, Sanders co, Nebraska.
Lauer, W C L, Gorham, Ontario co, N Y.
Laufer, M F, Leetonia, Colum co, Ohio.
Lauritzen, J R, New London,Waupaca co,Wis.
Lautenschlager, J, Ashland, Boyd co, Ky.
Lautenschlager, J F, Hausertown, Ind.
Lauterbach, O, Lonaconing, Allegheny co,Md.
Lavender, G E, Milner Station, Ga.
*Lawrence, D W, Avoca, Cicero, Onond co,NY.
*Lawson, S S, Freeport, Stephenson co, Ills.
Lawson, J S, Zollarsville, Wash'n co, Pa.
*Lazarus, R, Grantville, Alleghany co, Md.
*Leathers, A. Claremont, Richland co, Ills.
*Leddin, F, Mellenville, Columbia co, N Y.
Ledebur, F, Bath, Mason co, Ills.
*Lee, G A, Smicksburg, Indiana co. Pa.
Leemhuis, E, North East, Erie co, Pa.
*Leeser, J II, Gettysburg, Pa.
*Lefler, J, Berne. Albany co, N Y.
Lehman, A, Des Peres, St Louis co, Mo.
Lehman, E, New Wells, Cape Girardeau co,Mo
Lehmann, Prof W F, Columbus, Ohio.
Lehman, F F O, Chicago, Ills.
Lehner, Jas, New Haven, Allen co, Ind.
Cehrer, J G, Sandusky city, Ohio.
*Leisher, G W, New Wilm'n, Lawrence co,Pa
Leist, J, Camp Charlotte, Pickaway co, Ohio.
*Leiter G, Congress, Wayne co, Ohio.
*Leitzell, D W, Sligo, Clarion co, Pa.
Lembke, W C, Marysville, Union co, Ohio.
Lembke, C H C, New Bedford, Coshocton co, O.
Lemcke, II J II, W Newton, Westm'ld co, Pa.
Lemke, II, Manistee, Mich.

Lenk, E O, St Louis, Mo.
Lenker, M B, Lykens, Dauphin co, Pa.
*Lentz, A W, Woodsboro', Frederick co, Md.
*Lentz, A S, Liverpool, Perry co, Pa.
Lenz, J, Edgerton, Williams co, Ohio.
Leonberger, J, Milville, Cumberland co, N J.
Leopold, O, Orefield, Lehigh co, Pa.
*Lepley, C, Beckleyville, Carroll co, Md.
Les·mann, W, Sherrill's Mound, Iowa.
Letterman, A, Yorktown, Dewitt co, Texas.
Leupp, A, Franklin Mills, Des Mo's co, Iowa.
Leyhe, J J F, Grand Rapids, Wood co,Wis.
Lieb, C C, ——, Iowa.
Lieb, J G, Brenham, Washington co, Texas.
Liebe, C F, Sakeville, Randolph co, Ills.
Liefeld, A, Caledonia Centre, Racine co, Wis.
Liese, S, Quincy, Adams co, Ills.
*Leitzell, D W, Curllsville, Clarion co, Pa.
Lilje, C, Galion, Ohio.
Lill·soe, J P, Muskegon, Mich.
*Lilly, A W, York, York co, Pa.
*Lilly, N W, Dixon, Lee co, Ills.
*Lilly, W II, Bellefonte, Centre co, Pa.
*Lindahl, P A S, Galesburg, Ill.
*Lindahl, C J, Brantford, Kansas.
Lindahl, —, Laporte, Ind.
Lindahl, S P A, Galesburg, Knox co, Ills.
Lindahl, C P A, Woodhull, Ills.
Lindberg, C E, 216 Franklin st, Philadel, Pa.
Lindeblad, H O,Chandler's Val,Warren co, Pa.
Lindell, C O, Geneva, Lane co, Ills.
Lindemann, F, Decorah, Winneshiek co, Iowa.
Lindemann,Prof J C W,Addison,Du Page, Ills.
Lindh, L O, Marine, Washington co, Minn.
Lindholm, A, Altona, Knox co, Ills.
Lindler, A W, Leesville, S C.
Linell, T O, Lawrence, Kansas.
*Lingle, J M, Grandview, Spencer co, Ind.
Link, G, St Louis, Mo.
*Link, J II, Edinburg, Johnson co, Ind.
*Linker, R G, Liberty, Adams co, Ills.
Linsenmann, W, Fisherville, Haldim co, Ont.
*Linstz, Aug, Lock Haven, Clinton co, Pa.
*Lipe, L L, Mt Morris, Ogle co, Ills.
*Lipe, W A, Omaha, Nebraska.
Li·t, J A, St Sebald, Clayton co. Iowa.
List, J, Roseville, Macomb co, Mich.
Little, M L, Lincolnton, Lincoln co, N C.
*Livengood, J, Butler, Montgom'y co, Ills.
Lizner, W A, Jonesborough, Ga.
*Lochman, A H, DD, York, Pa.
Lochner, F, Milwaukee, Wis.
Lochner, L, Richmond, Va.
*Locker, P, Salamonia, Jay co, Ind.
Loeber, G S, Niles, Cook co, Ills.
Loeber, H, Milwaukee, Wis.
*Loeffler, Gottlieb, Ackley, Hardin co, Iowa.
Loewenstein, G, Richmond, Wayne co, Ind.
Lohr, G A, Clarinda, Page co, Iowa.
Lohrmann, C, Richmond, Macomb co, Mich.
Long, A J, Stouchsburg, Berks co, Pa.
Long, G J, Canfield, Mahoning co, Ohio.
Long, G A, Smithfield, Va.
*Long, II F, Arendtsville, Adams co, Pa.
Long, J M, East Germantown, Wayne co, Ind.
Loszner, F A H, Beecher, Will co, Ill.
Lothmann, H W, Akron, Ohio.
Lowman, J B, Lexington C H, S C.
Loy, Prof Matthias, Columbus, Ohio.
Lubkert, W C H, Butler, Pa.
Lukas, P, Beaver Dam, Dodge co, Wis.
*Luckenbach,W H, Hagerst'n,Wash'n co, Md.
*Ludden,A P,Centre Brunswick, Ren'r co,N Y

Lucker, C H, Aroma, Dickinson co, Kansas.
Luescher, ——, Aldboro', Ont.
Lundahl, G, La Porte, La Porte co, Ind.
Lundblad,J P, Parker's Prairie,Otter co, Minn.
Lund, L, Leavenworth, Brown co, Minn.
Lunde, A, Utica, Dane co, Wis.
Lutz, A F, Monroe, Monroe co, Mich.
Lutz, Prof F, Galena, Jo Daviess co, Ill.
Luz, H, Dubuque, Iowa.
Lysnes, D, Decorah, Winneshiek co, Iowa.

Maack, H, Sugar Grove, Fairfield co, Ohio.
Maas, C T, Hudson City, N J.
*Mack, P S, Hummelstown, Dauphin co, Pa.
Mackensen, W, Hanover, Grey co, Ontario.
Madsen, N, New Denmark, Brown co, Minn.
Maeurer, C, Grayville, White co, Ills.
*Magee, Irving, DD, Albany, N Y.
Magelsen, C, Orfordville, Rock co, Wis.
Magelsen, K, Bratsberg, Fillmore co, Minn.
Magnus, M, Arendal, Fillmore co, Minn.
Magnuson, C J, Lake Station, Lake co, Ind.
Magny, J, Cannon Falls, Goodhue co, Minn.
Mahlberg E, Breakneck, Butler co, Pa.
Mahnberg, J C, Geneseo, Henry co, Ills.
Mahood, J, Burkes Garden, Tazewell co,Va.
*Maier, L D, 94 E Fayette st, Baltimore. Md.
*Mallinson,M,Minnieska,Wabashow co,Minn.
Maisch, J M, Paola, Miami co, Kansas.
Malmberg, J, Geneseo, Henry co, Ills.
Mangelsdorf, L E, Bloomington, McL co, Ills.
*Manges, E, Luthersburg, Clearfield co, Pa.
Mann, Prof W J, DD, 228 Franklin st, Phila-
    delphia, Pa.
*Mann, L A, Burkittsville, Frederick co, Md.
Manning, J, Deavertown, Morgan co, Ohio.
Manz, G, Lyons, Wayne co, N Y.
*Marcley,ODS, Orleans 4 Corners, Jeff co, N Y.
Margart, J P, Eufaula, Barbour co, Ala.
Markhus, L J, Kandiyohi, Minn.
Markworth, E G C, Weyauwega,Waup co,Wis.
Markworth, G, Wyandotte, Wayne co, Mich.
*Martenis, A, Maryland, Otsego co, N Y.
Martens, D M, Tyrone, Blair co, Pa.
Martens, M, Sterling, Johnson co, Neb.
Martin, Prof Adam,Gettysburg, Adams co,Pa.
*Martin, Prof C, M D, St Joseph, Buch co, Mo.
*Martin, E H, Dansville, Livingston, co, N Y.
Martin, J C H, New Bremen, Cook co, Ills.
*Martz, G J, Womelsdorf, Berks co, Pa.
Maschopp, G S, ——
Matshat, P, Plymouth, Wayne co, Mich.
Matter F, Des Moines, Iowa.
Mattfeld, T, N Lizard, Pocahontas co, Iowa.
*Matthis, F A, West Cairo, Allen co, Ohio.
Matthias, J, Marysville, Marshall co, Kansas.
Matuschka, F W G,New Melle,St Chas co, Mo.
Mayer, C, Kellerville, Dubois co, Ind.
Mayer, C C, San Antonio, Texas.
Mayerhoff. E. West Bend, Washington co,Wis.
Mayser, Fred P, Lancaster, Pa.
*McAfee, J B, Topeka, Kansas.
*McAtee. J Q,Chambersburg, Franklin co, Pa.
*McCullough, A W, Parkwood, Indiana co, Pa.
McClanahan, W S, Salem, Roanoke co, Va.
*McCron, Prof John, DD, Hagerstown, Md.
McDaniel, R E, Piedmont, W Va.
McDonald, B H, Wytheville, Wythe co, Va.
*McHenry, S, Huntingdon, Pa.
McKee, David, Greenville, Mercer co, Pa.
*McKenzie, David L, Frostb'g, Alleg'y co,Md
*McKnight, H W, Easton, Northam'n co, Pa.
*McLaughlin,A,White Pigeon,St Jos co,Mich.

*McReynolds, S, Kokomo, Howard co, Ind.
Mechling, G W, Lancaster, Ohio.
Meerwein, O, Wheeling, W Va.
Mees, C, Columbus, Ohio.
Meiser, G F H,Youngstown, Mahoning co, O.
Meier, T, Custar, Wood co, O.
Meissner,T J, Reynolds Stat'n, White co,Ind.
Meissner, J M, Punxatawney, Jeffs'n co, Pa.
Melgren, C P, Osage City, Osage co, Kansas.
Melhorn, J K, Pittsburg, south side, Pa.
Mellander, J., Warren, Warren co, Pa.
Mellbye, O A, New Richland, Minn.
*Mengert, J H, Baltimore, Md.
*Menges, J H, York, York co, Pa.
Mennicke, C A, Rock Island, Ills.
*Mennig, Wm G, Allentown, Lehigh co, Pa.
Mertens, Th, Fort Dodge, Webster co, Iowa.
Merz, H, Rutersville, Fayette co, Texas.
Merz, M, Brownstown, Jackson co, Ind.
Metzger, C, Hopkins Station,Allegan co, Mich.
Metzler, E J, Gettysburg, Pa.
Meumann, Dr T, Fond du Lac, Wis.
Meyer, A, Houston, Texas.
Meyer, C A, Danvers, McLean co, Ills.
Meyer, C F, Zumbrota, Goodhue co, Minn.
Meyer, C F H, East St Louis, Ills.
Meyer, H, Lincoln, Logan co, Ills.
Meyer, H, Kirchhayn, Washington Co, Wis.
Meyer, H, Detroit, Mich.
Meyer, J G, Burlington, Racine co, Wis.
Meyer, J, Fort Atkinson,Winneshiek co,Iowa.
Meyer, M, Leavenworth, Kansas.
Meyer, W L, Pomeroy, Meigs co, Ohio.
Michael, M, Hamburg, Erie co, N Y.
Michaellis, A, Monroe, Monroe co, Mich.
Michels, H E, Canaan, Gasconade co, Mo.
Middleswarth, A B, Orangeville, Ills.
Mieszler, T, Cole Camp, Benton co, Mo.
Mieszler, B, Palmyra, Marion co, Mo.
Mikkelsen, A, 256 W Ind st, Chicago, Ills.
*Miller, A B, Liberty, Tioga co, Pa.
*Miller, A S, Manorville, Armstrong co, Pa.
Miller, C P, Upper Black's Eddy,Bucks co,Pa.
*Miller, Elijah, Jonesboro', Union co, Ills.
*Miller, Ephraim, Dixon, Lee co, Ills.
Miller, F A, Zyster, Wis.
Miller, Prof G F, Allentown, Lehigh co, Pa.
*Miller, Geo W, Findlay, Hancock co, Ohio.
*Miller, Henry B, Galion, Crawford co, Ohio.
Miller, H S, Phœnixville, Chester Co, Pa.
*Miller, John, Columbia city, Whitley co,Ind.
*Miller, J B, Minerva, Stark co, Ohio.
Miller, J C, Knoxville, Knox co, Tenn.
Miller, Prof J I, Staunton, Augusta co, Va.
Miller, J Jay, Baton Rouge, La.
*Miller, J K, Centre Hall, Centre co, Pa.
Miller, J W, New Haven, Mason co, W Va.
*Miller, J W, Linn Grove, Adams co, Ind.
Miller, L G M, N Wales, Montg'y co, Pa.
*Miller, Paul, Carolina, Ohio.
Miller, Peter, Concord, N C.
Miller, P H, German Settlement, W Va.
*Miller, S S, Lairdsville, Lycoming co, Pa.
Miller, T, Edenburg, Shenandoah co, Va.
*Miller, Val, Farnham, Erie co, N Y.
*Miller, Victor, Clearspring, Wash co, Md.
Minnich, M R, Staunton, Va.
Moegle, J, Wesley, Texas.
Moedinger, C G, New Orleans, La.
Moeller, F A, Urne's Corner, Buffalo co, Wis.
Mochel, G, Shelbyville, Shelby co, Ills.
Mohn, T N, St Paul, Minn'a.
Mohr, G, Holland, Dubois co, Ind.

Mohrhoff,'H W, Chatfield, Ohio.
Moldehnke, Dr Ed, 124 E 46th st, N York City
Moll, J M M, Lansing, Mich.
Moll, K L, Detroit, Mich.
*Moore, Geo E, Seville, Ohio.
Moretz, C, Boone, Watauga co, N C.
Morgan, Jesse, Sallis, Attala co, Miss.
*Morris, John G, DD, Baltimore, Md.
*Morris, J N, Columbia City,Whitley co, Ind.
*Morrison, M S, Monroeville,Clinton co, Ind.
Moses, J T, Spilville, Winneshiek co, Iowa.
Moser, A D L, Frog Level,Newberry co, N C.
*Moser, D M, Gettysburg, Adams co, Pa.
Moser, J C, China Grove, Rowan co, N C.
Moser, J R, Gravelton, Wayne co, Mo.
Moser, T, Mt Pleasant, Cabarrus co, N C.
Mueller, C R O, Ashland, Ohio.
Mueller, G A, Kankakee city, Ills.
Mueller, HJ,Willow Cr'k, Blue Earth co,Minn.
Mueller, J, Wolcottsville, N Y.
Mueller, J A F W, Johnsburg, Pa.
Mueller, J F, Frankenlust, Saginaw co, Mich.
*Mueller, J G, 1144 4th st, Philadelphia, Pa.
Mueller, Lewis, DD, Charleston, S C.
Mueller, P H, Trenton, Ohio.
Muenzinger, J N, Phillipsburg, Ontario.
Muhlenberg, Prof F A, DD, Allentown, Pa.
Mulhauser, J, Zelienople, Butler co, Pa.
Muller, A H, Council Bluffs, Iowa.
Multanowsky, E, Waterford, Racine co, Wis.
Mumme, T, Sequin, Guadaloupe co, Texas.
Munsh, S, Eakin, Allegheny co, Pa.
Mutschmann, F, Edon, Williams co, Ohio.
Muus, B J, Norway, Goodhue co, Minna.
*Myers, A, Salem, Marion co, Oregon.
Myers, E, Jewett, Cumberland co, Ills.
*Myers, J C, Indianapolis, Ind.
Myers, J W, Bakersville, Coshocton co, Ohio.
*Myers, U, Turbotville, Northumb'd co, Pa.

Nabholz, L, Hallowaysville, Bureau co, Ills.
Nachtigall, J, Waterloo, Monroe co, Ills.
Naessa, O, Brule, Union co, Dakota.
Naesz, O, Dodgeville, Iowa co, Wis.
Neuthardt, A, Round Top, Fayette co, Texas.
*Neff, J P, Montoursville, Lycoming co, Pa.
*Neff, George, Rhinebeck, Duchess co, N Y.
Neff, Jacob, Spring City, Chester co, Pa.
Neiffer, Jac G, Salisbury, Rowan co, N. C.
Neiman, J H, Conyngham, Luzerne co, Pa.
*Nellis, P S, Eaton, Crawford co, Ills.
Nelson, M, Pecatonia, Winnebago co, Ills.
Nething, J, Junction City, Kansas.
Neumann, Robert, Box 5296, New York City.
Neuthardt, A, Round Top, Fayette co, Texas.
Neutzel, J G F, Marysville, Union co, Ohio.
Neutzel, J G, Columbus, Bartholo'w co, Ind.
*Nicholls, H, East Worcester, Otsego co, N Y.
Nielsen,A S, Cedar Falls, Blk. Hawk co,Iowa.
Nielson, A, Omaha, Nebraska.
Niemann, H, Little Rock, Ark.
Niethammer, J F, La Porte, Ind.
Nietmann, Kewannee, Wis.
Nilson, J M, Pocatonica, Ills.
Nilson, J S, Waverly, Wright co, Minna.
*Nixdorff, G A, Georgetown, D C.
Noll, John C, Red Bud, Randolph co, Ills.
Nolte, C A, Stringtown, Cole co, Mo.
Nordgren, N, De Kalb, De Kalb co, Ills.
Norden, H, Pebble Creek, Dodge co, Neb.
Nordeck, E T, Woodbury, Wash'n co, Minna.
Norem, L H, Elk Mound, Dunn co, Wis.
Norman, O A, Sioux City, Iowa.

Norelius, E, Vasa, Goodhue co, Minna.
Notz, Prof N W A, Watertown, Wis.
*Nunemacher, J D, Millersburg, Ohio.
*Nuner, J A, Sculp Level, Cambria co, Pa.
Nuoffer, F J, Eagle Lake, Will co, Ills.
*Nye, R H, Arcadia, Hancock co, Ohio.
Nyquist, J P, 181 Burnell st, Chicago, Ills.

*O'Bannon, P N, Newark, Licking co, Ohio.
Obenschaine, J P, Lexington, Rockbr co, Va.
Obermeier, C, Farmington, St Franc co, Mo.
*Ochampaugh, C, Stokes, Oneida co, N Y.
Ochler, M, Myersville, De Witt co, Texas.
Oehlert, G, Nauvoo Hancock co, Ills.
Oehlschlaeger, C J, Chillicothe, Ross co, O.
Oesterberg, S J, Kansas City, Mo.
Oestermeyer,F W,St Johns'g,Niagara co,N Y
Oetjen, J J, Monticello, Jones co, Iowa.
Oetjens, J, Toledo, Ohio.
Oetting, W C H, Lindenwood, Ogle co, Ills.
Oftedahl, Prof S, Minneapolis, Minn.
Ohl, J F, Quakertown, Bucks co, Pa.
Olsen, A C, Pilot Centre, Kankakee co, Ills.
Olsen, E, Canton, Lincoln co. Dakota.
*Olsen, G, New Denmark, Wis.
Olsen, II, Swedesburg, Henry co, Iowa.
Olsen, J, St. Ansgar, Mitchell co, Iowa.
Olsen, Nils, Owatonna, Steele co, Minn.
Olsen, Ole, Anderson, Burnett co, Wis.
Olson, O, Lindsborg, McPherson co, Kansas.
Opitz, A, Schleissingerville, Wis.
Oppen, C E, Columbus. Columbia co, Wis.
*Ort, M, Lockport, Niagara co, N Y.
*Ort, S A, Louisville, Ky.
*Orwig, S P, Watsontown, Northum'd co,Pa.
Ostby, G P, Lille Cedar, Minn.
Osterberg, S J, Kansas City, Mo.
Osterhus, L, Dubuque, Iowa.
*Oswald, Jonathan, DD, York, Pa.
*Oswald, Solomon, York, Pa.
Ottesen, J A, Utica, Dane, Wis.
Ottman, Fr, Collinsville, Madison co, Ills.
*Owen, S W, Hagerstown, Wash'n co, Md.

*Palmer, S S,Chester Springs,Chester co, Pa.
*Paltzgroff, N, Canton, Stark co, Ohio.
Parker, E P, Brick Church, Guilford co, N C.
*Parson, Geo, Hanover, York co, Pa.
*Parson, Prof W E, Japan.
Partenfelder, H, Bay City, Bay co, Mich.
Pasavant, W A, DD, Pittsburgh, Pa.
Paulsen, I K, Rajahmunary, India.
Paulsen, O, Wilmar. Minn.
*Pearce, N B, Marble Hill, Tenn.
Pedersen, J, Lusck, Polk co, Wis.
Pehrson, J, Norseland, Nicollet co, Minn.
*Pehrssen, G A, Boston, Mass.
Pennekamp, F W, Bremen, Randolph co, Ills.
*Peschau, F W E, Evansville, Ind.
*Peter, Jacob, Manheim, Lancaster co, Pa.
Peter, P A, W Baltimore, Mont'y co, Ohio.
*Peters, G N H, Springfield, Clark co, Ohio.
Peters, Gustav, Rockford,Winnebago co, Ills.
Peters, H, Columbus, Ohio.
Petersen, Prof C J P, Decorah, Iowa.
Petersen, F, Mooer's Prairie,Wright co, Minn.
Petersen, J C J, Booneville, Oneida co, N Y.
Peterson, John, Des Moines, Iowa.
Peterson, J R, Dallas, Gaston co, N C,
*Pfahler, M F, Elk Lick, Somerset co, Pa.
Pfatteicher, P, Easton, Northampton co, Pa.
Pfeiffer, L, Seneca, Nemaha co, Kansas.
Pfenning W, Zionsville, Wash'ton co, Texas.

Pfenninger, H, Berlin,Washington co, Texas.
Pfister, A, Germanville, Jefferson co, Iowa.
Pfuhl, J G, Steubenville, Jefferson co, Ohio.
Phillippi, Alex. Wytheville,Wythe co, Va.
Pihlgren, P. A, Fort Dodge, Iowa.
*Pile, G M, Salesburg, Somerset co, Pa.
Pissel, T, Matteson, Cook co, Ills.
*Pitcher, Prof J, Hartwick Sem'y,Ots co, NY.
*Plambeck, Chr, Arenzville, Cass co, Ills.
Plehn, G, Chippewa Falls, Wis.
Plitt, J K, Catasauqua, Lehigh co, Pa.
Poeverlein, L, ——, Iowa.
*Poffenberger, J W, Gettysburg, Pa.
Pohl, A, Bernhards Mills, Butler co, Pa.
Pohlmann, F W, Lanesville, Harrison co, Ind.
Polack, G, Cape Girardeau, Mo.
Poorman, A, Farmersville,Montgomery co,O.
Popp, C, Kenosha, Wis.
Poppen, S, New Dundee, Waterloo co, Ont.
*Porr, Wm S, Brickerville, Lancaster co, Pa.
*Porter, Ira S,Breakabean, Schoharie co, N Y.
Potter, J Newton, Hamilton, Mifflin co, Pa.
*Pracht, C O II, Norristown, Montg'y co, Pa
Prager, G, Good Hope, Milwaukee co, Wis.
Preller, A, Galena, Ills.
Preus, Herman A, Leeds, Columbia co, Wis.
*Price, N M, 1646 Franklin st, Philadelp'a,Pa.
*Prince, Prof B F, Springfield, Clark co,Ohio.
Princell, J G. 324 E 21st st, New York, N Y.
*Pritchard, C, Barren Hill, Mont'y co, Pa.
Probst, C, Alpena, Mich.
*Probst, G C, Everett, Bedford co, Pa.
*Probst, J F, Gettysburg, Adams co, Pa.
Proehl, H, Darmstadt, St Clair co, Ills.
Proehl, H F, Durand, Pepin co, Wis.
Proft. J, Giddings. Lee co, Texas.
Prottengeier, Ch, Toledo, Ohio.

Quammen, N, Christiania, Dakota co, Minn.
Quehl, Helidor W, Manitowoc, Wis.
Querl, H W, Toledo, Ohio.
Quern, G H W, Middle Village, L Island. N Y.

*Raby, P, Kimberton, Chester Co, Pa.
Rader, Andrew, Brush Creek, Mo.
Rademacher, G, Bird's Hill, Carroll co, Md.
Raedeke, H, Carver, Carver co, Minna.
Raegener, H, 101 7th st, New York city.
Rahn, S S, Atlanta, Ga.
Raible, J, Kalamazoo, Mich.
*Raisig, J J, Fryburg, Clarion co, Pa
Ramelow, H, Prairietown, Ills.
Ranseen, M C, Elgin, Kane co, Ills.
*Rasback, J, Orleans 4 Corners. Jeff'n co,N Y.
Rasmussen, P A, Lisbon, Kendall co, Ills.
*Rath, A B, Schoolcraft, Kalamazoo co,Mich.
Rath, J B, Bethlehem,, Northampton co, Pa.
Rath, Wm, Allentown, Lehigh co, Pa.
Rathjen, H, Mayville, Dodge co, Wis.
Raths, C, Hartford, Ottawa co. Ohio.
Rausch, G, Middleburg, Cuyahoga co, Ohio.
Rauschert, J, Dalton, Cook co, Ills.
Raw, J Leonard, Flint, Genesee co, Mich.
Rechenberg, C F W, Montreal, Ont.
Reck, Prof H, Paxton, Ford co, Ills.
Reck, M, Spring Valley, Fillmore co, Minn.
Recker, A, Havana, Mason co, Ills.
*Reed,D E, McKee's Half Falls, Snyder co,Pa.
Reed, E I, Trenton, N J.
*Rees, Jas M, Freeport, Stephenson co, Ills.
*Reese, E S, Lisbon, Linn co, Iowa.
*Reese, J W, North Hope, Butler co, Pa.
Rebkopf, —, Osseo, Hennepin co, Minn.

Rehn, A, Malcolm, Poweshiek co, Iowa.
Rehn, A H, Muscoda, Grant co, Wis.
Rehnstroem, J E, 4 Corners, Jeff'n co, Iowa.
Rehwinkel, W, Jenny, Marathon co, Wis.
Rehwoldt, H, Sauk City, Sauk co, Wis.
Reichardt, G, Columbia City, Whitley co,Ind.
Reichenbecher, Chr. Plattville, Grant co,Wis.
Reichert, G A, Kittanning, Armstr'ng co, Pa.
Reichert, C G. Grove City, Franklin co, Ohio.
Reichmann, F H, News, Calhoun co, Ills.
Reidenbach, PM, Evansv'e,Vanderb'h co, Ind.
Reiff, G, Marion, Marion co, Ohio.
Reimann, H J, Wabash, Ind.
*Reimensnyder, C, Lancaster, Pa.
*Reimensnyder, J M, Espy, Columbia co, Pa.
Reimensnyder, J B, Savannah, Ga.
Reim, C G, La Crosse, Wis.
Reim, G. New Ulm, Brown co, Minn.
Rein, G W, Osgood, Ripley co, Ind.
Reinhardt, F A, Bethalto, Madison co, Ills.
Reinke, A, Chicago, Ills.
*Reinmund, J F, Lebanon, Lebanon co, Pa.
Reinsch, B, Cole Camp, Benton co, Mo.
Reinsch, G, Janesville, Rock co, Wis.
Reisinger, Geo, Danville, Vermillion co, Ills.
Reitz, G F, Arlington, Hancock co, Ohio.
*Reitz, J G, Hagerstown, Washing'n co, Md.
*Rembold, J, Andrew, Jackson co, Iowa.
Rennicke, J, Wayside, Brown co, Wis.
Renninger, J S, Schnecksville, Lehigh co,Pa.
Renz, J C, Hudson, Columbia co, N Y.
Repass, J C, Rural Retreat, Wythe co, Va.
Repass, Prof S A, Salem, Roanoke co, Va.
Reque, P S, Gilchrist, Pope co, Minn.
Reque, S S, Spring Grove, Houston co, Minn.
Reuschel, C, Mitchell, Perth co, Ont.
Reuther, H, Ann Arbor, Mich.
Reuther, W, Bay City, Bay co, Mich.
*Rhodes, G M, Bedford, Bedford co, Pa.
*Rhodes, M, Wash'n st , St Louis, Mo.
Rhudy, S, Thompson's Valley. Tazew'l co,Va.
*Rice, J M, Belleville, Mifflin co, Pa.
*Rice, Levi, Corunna, De Kalb co, Ind.
Richards, Frank, 117 N. Sixth st, Phila, Pa.
*Richard,Prof Jas W,Carthage,Hanc'k co,Ills
Richards, Matthias H, Indianapolis, Ind.
*Richardson, X J,Smithsburg,Wash'n co,Md.
Richman, F W, Elgin, Winnebago co, Ills.
Richter, E T, Dorsey, Ills.
Richter, F L, M D, Minneapolis, Minn.
Rickert, W H, Williamsport, Pa.
*Ridenour, S, Hickory, Van Buren co, Iowa.
Rieb, W, 140 Court street, Newark, N J.
Riedel, C R, Hillsboro', Jefferson co, Mo.
Riedel, E, Homewood, Cook co, Ills.
*Rietz, G L, Washington, D C.
*Rightmyer, P M, Cohansey, Cumb'd co,N J.
Riis, H N, Schleswig Holstein, Germany.
Ritter, J, McWilliams Precinct, Nebraska.
*Rizer, P, Stewartsville, Warren co, N J.
Roeder, J E, Dunton Station, Cook co, Ills.
Roehm, F C, Frelsburg, Colorado co. Texas.
Roelle, J H, Benson, Woodford co, Ills.
Roeller, Isaac, Kutztown, Berks co, Pa.
Roernaes, H, Ishpeming, Marquette co,Mich.
Roesch, Tobias, Ten Mile House, Wis.
*Rogers, H M, S Wellfleet, Barnst'e co, Mass.
Rohe, C H, Joliet. Will co, Ills.
Rohrlack, A, Reedsburg, Sauk co, Wis.
Rolf, E, St Paul, Minn.
*Roller, W B, Greenford, Ohio.
Roof, J A, Jewett, Harrison co, Ohio.
Rosenberg, F Von, ———, Germany.

*Rosenberg, J A, Hudson, Columbia co, N Y.
*Rosenmiller. D P, Lancaster, Pa.
Rosenstand, H, Mainstee, Mich.
Rosenwinkel, G, Wausau, Marathon co, Wis.
Rosholdt, T, Elizabeth City, Minn.
Ross, D C, Newcastle, Henry co, Ind.
Roth, Prof II W, Greenville. Mercer co, Pa.
*Roth, Fred, Big Springs, Douglass co, Kan.
*Roth, G, Chambersburg, Franklin co, Pa.
Roth, J D, Scenery Hill, Washington co, Pa.
Rothacker, D, Doylestown, Ohio.
Rothrock, S, Salisbury, Rowan co, N C.
*Roths, G, Beardstown, Snyder co, Pa.
*Rowe, A D, Guntur, India.
Rude, A R. DD, Columbia, S C.
Rudi, C C, Black Jack Springs, Texas.
Ruediger, W, Augusta, Eau Claire co, Wis.
*Rueter, C A, Fontenelle,Wash'n co, Neb.
Ruether, H, Ann Arbor. Mich.
Ruff, F J, St Clair, St Clair co, Mich.
Ruh ,M P, Hartland, Waukesha co. Mich.
Ruhland, C F T, Germany.
Rumple, J W, Lancaster, Pa.
Runkel, G, Aurora, Dearborn co, Ind.
Ruperti, J, DD, 130 Elizabeth st,N York, N Y.
Rupprecht, F K, Norfolk, Madison co, Neb.
Rupprecht, J, North Dover, Cuyahoga co, O.
Rupprecht, P, Hutchinson, McLeod co, Minn
Russmisel, Wm, Lebanon, Russell co, Va.
Rustad, L O, Norway Lake, Monon'a co, Minn.
*Ruth, F J, Galion, Crawford co. Ohio.
*Ruthrauff, J M, Circleville, Pickaway co, O.
Ruthrauff, W P, Zanesville. Muskin'm co, O.
Ryden, C M, Bernadotte, Nicollet co, Minn.
*Ryder, D L, Hollidaysburg, Blair co, Pa.
*Ryder, J W, Republic, Seneca co, Ohio.
Rydholm, C P, Burlington, Iowa.

*Sadtler, Prof B, DD,Lutherville, Balt co,Md.
Saether, H E. Ewald, Faribault co, Minn.
*Sagehorn, H, Berlin, Ontario.
*Sahm, Peter, DD, New Berlin, Union co, Pa.
Salinger, J, Elmira, Waterloo co, Ontario.
Sallman, C, Newburg, Cuyahoga, co, Ohio.
*Saltsman, P G, North Georgetown, Wis.
Sampson, M, Taylor Station, Jackson co,Wis.
Sandvosz, W, Port Hudson, Franklin co, Mo.
Sandell, M, Sweden.
*Sanders. C W, Fairview, Fulton co, Ills.
Sando, O O, St Olaf, Minnehaha co, Dak.
Sangstedt. C, Trysild, Minn.
Sanner, Daniel, Tremont, Schuylkill co, Pa.
Sanngren, J M, 322 N Market st, Chicago,Ills
Sannquist, P M, Woodhull, Henry co, Ills.
Sans, C, Joliet, Ills.
Sappenfield, J M G, Waveland, Montg co,Ind.
Sapper, C F W, St Louis, (Carondelet), Mo.
*Sargent, F W, Eureka, Greenw'd co, Kansas.
Sarver, Jonat'n, Leechburg, Armstr'g co, Pa.
Sauer, H G, Mobile, Ala.
Sauer, J G, Dudleytown. Jackson co, Ind.
Sauer, J J, Elias, N Leeds, Columbia co, Wis.
Sauer, M, St Louis, Mo.
Sauer, O A, Fort Dodge. Webster co, Iowa.
Saugstad, C, Holmes City, Douglass co,Minn.
Saupert, A, Evansville, Vanderburg co. Ind.
Schaaf, G P A, Lewiston, Winona co. Minn.
Schadegg, J, Prescott, Pierce co, Wis.
Schadow, C, Rosenkranz, Manitowoc co, Wis.
Schaechter, H A, Dudleytown, Jack'n co,Ind.
Schaeffer, Prof C F, DD, 1204 Mt Vernon st, Philadelphia, Pa.
Schaeffer, Prof C W, DD, Germantown, Pa.

*Schaeffer, G F, Somerset, Somerset co, Pa.
*Schaeffer, Geo W, Le Claire, Scott co, Iowa.
Schaeffer, J, Lagrange. Ind.
Schaefer, J G, New Boston, Spencer co, Ind.
Schaeffer, J G, Piqua, Miami co, Ohio.
Schaeffer, W A, Easton, Northampton co, Pa.
*Schaeffer, W C, Grafton, Taylor co, W Va.
Schaller, F, Redbud, Randolph co, Ills.
Schaller, Prof G, St Louis, Mo.
Schambach, G, Sullivan, Gray co, Ont.
Schantz, F J F, Myerstown, Lebanon co, Pa.
*Schauer, J, Gambier, Knox co, Ohio.
Scheleen, C J, Bismarck, Waubaunsee, Kan.
Scheldahl, O, Cambridge, Story co, Iowa.
Scheie, A A, Newburg, Fillmore co, Minn.
*Schell, Levi, West Camp, Ulster co, N Y.
Schepstedt. A G, Essex, Page co, Iowa.
*Scherer, A H, Sharpsville, Tipton co, Ind.
*Scherer, F R, Waterville, Marshall co, Kan.
Scherer, Prof J J, Marion, Smythe co, Va.
Scherer, Simeon, Gibsonville, Guilford co, N C.
Scherven, L, Osses, Tempeleau co. Wis.
*Scheurer, P, Hanover, York co, Pa.
Scheurer, J F. Bellefontaine, Logan co, O.
Schick, Prof Geo, Fort Wayne, Ind.
Schiedt, F, Alleghany city, Pa.
Schieferdecker. G A, Ottawa, Monroe co, Mich.
Schierenbeck. Prof J H C, Walhalla, Oc co, S C.
Schilling, G F, Auburn, Fond du Lac co, Wis.
Schilling, W C, ——
Schillinger, B F, Petersburg, Mahoning co, O.
Schimmel, C. Hamilton, Ontario.
Schimpf, M, Mahanoy City. Schuylkill co, Pa.
Schimpf, W, Woodland, Dodge co, Wis.
Schindel, Jacob D, Allentown, Lehigh co, Pa.
*Schindler, Daniel, Adrian, Mich.
Schlechte, F W, Strasburg, Shelby co, Ills.
*Schlene, C J, Bismarck, Kansas.
Schlesselman. H, Arcadia, Hamilton co, Ind.
Schlenker, C, Toledo, Ohio.
Schliepsick, C H G, Cayuga, Liv'ston co, Ills.
*Schloegel, C A, Baltimore, Md.
*Schmalzl, J, Cullman, Blount co, Ala.
Schmauk, B W, Lebanon, Lebanon co, Pa.
Schmeiser, J, Burlington, Iowa.
Schmid, Prof E, Columbus, Ohio.
Schmid. Black Jack Springs, Texas.
Schmidt, C, Warren, Trumbull co, Ohio.
Schmidt, C E, Elyria, Lorain co, Ohio.
Schmidt, F, Ann Arbor, Mich.
Schmidt, Prof F A, St Louis, Mo.
Schmidt, G A, Ward's Island, N York City.
Schmidt. H, Schaumburg, Cook co, Ills.
Schmidt, H A, Hubbard, Trumbull co, Ohio.
Schmidt, H C, Missionary in India.
Schmidt, Prof H I, DD, New York city.
Schmidt, H O, Lisbon, Kent co, Mich.
Schmidt, Jos, Saginaw City, Mich.
Schmidt, Jno C, Mahanoy, Northum'd co, Pa.
Schmidt, J H, Whitehaven, Luzerne co, Pa.
Schmidt, J J, Detroit, Mich.
Schmidt, P, Round Prairie, Todd co, Minn.
Schmidt, P, Skeel's X Roads, Mercer co, O.
Schmidt, Ph, Liverpool, Medina co, Ohio.
Schmidt, S, Chicago, Ills.
*Schmitt, C, Orwigsburg, Schuylkill co, Pa.
Schmitt, F W, Reserve, Erie co, N Y.
Schmogrow, G, Goshen, Elkhart co, Ind.
Schmogrow P G, Covington, Miami co, Ohio.
Schmogrow, W, St Mary's, Auglaize co, Ohio.
Schmolz, O, Genoa, Livingston co, Mich.
Schmucker, B M, DD, Reading, Pa.
Schmucker, Geo W, Philadelphia, Pa.

Schmucker, G, Upper Tract, Pendleton co, W Va.
Schneider, F, Concord, Jefferson co, Wis.
Schneider, J C, Metropolis City, Massac co, Ills.
Schneider, T, Waterloo, Ont.
*Schnur, Geo H, Bushnell, McDonough co, Ills.
*Schnur, J P, Macon, Macon co, Ills.
Schober, L C, Osage City, Cole Co, Mo.
Schoech, T, Pinckneyville, Perry co, Ills.
*Schoech, Wm H, Foreston, Ogle co, Ills.
*Schoemperlen, G H, Farview, Erie co, N Y.
Schoenberg, A, Burlington, Calhoun co, Mich.
Schoener, J P, Utica, N York.
*Scholl, Daniel, Lyons Station, Fayette co, Ind.
*Scholl, Geo, 332 W Lombard st, Balto, Md.
*Scholl, W N, DD, W Milton, Sara'o co, N Y.
Scholz, C F W, Corning, Holt co, Mo.
Schoeneberg, H, Lafayette, Ind.
*Schrader, —— M D, Keokuk Junction, Ills.
Schrader, C, Canton, Lewis co, Mo.
Schreckhise, J M, Moffatt's Creek, Va.
Schroeder, O, 424 Wharton st, Philadel'a, Pa.
Schroeppel, J A, Hillsdale, Mich.
Schroyer, W J, Johnsville, Montg co, Ohio.
Schroer, C A, Martinsville, Niagara co, N Y.
Schuette, Prof C H L, Columbus, Ohio.
Schuermann, E A, Homestead, Iowa co, Iowa.
Schuermer, J, Helen, McLeod co, Minn.
Schug, F, Wrightstown, Wis.
Schuh, H J, Canal Winchester, Ohio.
Schulenberg, J, Meriden, Steele co, Minn.
Schulz, A R, Bornholm, Perth co, Ontario.
Schulz, H, Neustadt, Grey co, Ont.
Schulze, A H, Fort Dodge, Webster co, Iowa.
Schulze, H A, Waynesburg, Stark co, Ohio.
Schulze, J A, Columbus, Ohio.
Schulze, J C, Ironton, Lawrence co, Ohio.
Schulze, K F, Cortland, Nicollet co, Minn.
Schueszler, A, Ballwin, St Louis co, Mo.
Schuetz, L, Ashebon, Dodge co, Wis.
Schumann, F, Freistadt, Ozankee co, Wis.
Schumacher, J, Caloma, Marion co. Iowa.
Schumm, G M, Willshire, Van Wert co, O.
Schuricht, Chas. Vandalia, Ills.
Schwan, C, Mt Clemens, Macomb co, Mich.
Schwan, H C, Cleveland, Ohio.
Schwan, Paul, Cleveland, Ohio.
Schwaemle, J G, Celina, Mercer co, Ohio.
Schwankehow, ——, Chicago, Ills.
Schwankowsky, C, Harrisburg, Pa.
*Schwartz, E, De Soto, Jackson co, Ills.
*Schwartz, JnoW, Worthing'n, Armstr'g co, Pa
Schwartz, W, White Rock, Huron co, Mich.
Schweigert, M, Kittanning, Armstrong co, Pa.
Schwensen, H J, Baden, St Louis co, Mo.
*Scivally, J, Marble Hill, Franklin co, Tenn.
Seachrist, A, Thomasville, Davidson co, N C.
Seachrist, S, Alliance, Ohio.
Seamad, C W, New York city.
*Secrist, L K, Wrightsville, York co, Pa.
Seeger, W F, Harlem, New York City, N Y.
Seibert, A F, Dayton, O.
Seidel, J, Maryville, Seward co, Minn'a.
*Seidel, W C, Davis, Stephenson co, Ills.
*Seifert, Henry, Jennertown, Somerset co, Pa.
Seifert, F. Stillwater, Washington co, Minn.
Seifert, F. Clayton, Centre, Iowa.
Seip, Prof Theod L, Allentown, Lehigh co, Pa.
Seippel, Prof —, Decorah, Winneshiek co, Iowa.
Seiss, J A, DD, 1338 Spring Garden st, Phil, Pa.
Seitz, C F, Avilla, Noble co, Ind.:
*Sell, D, New Kingston, Cumberland co, Pa.
Selle, Prof C A T, Addison, Du Page co, Ills.
Selleen, J, Randolph, Ripley co, Kansas,

Selleen, J O, Estherville, Emmitt co, Iowa.
*Selmser,J, Richmondville,Schoharie co,N Y.
*Senderling,J Z, DD,Johnst'n, Fulton co,N Y.
Seneker, J A, Midway, Greene co, Tenn.
Sencker, J E, New Hope, Augusta co, Va.
Senne, H C, Alma, Waubaunsee co, Kansas.
Serr, L, Montra, Shelby co, Ohio.
Sessler, J, Fairbank, Buchanan co, Iowa.
Setterdahl, A G, Moline, Ills.
Setterdahl, V, Orion, Henry co, Ills.
Setterdahl,S G,Campello, Plymouth co, Mass.
*Settlemoyer, G M, Des Moines, Polk co,Iowa.
*Settlemyer, W H, Wilmore, Cambria co, Pa.
Seuel, C, Mayville, Dodge co, Wis.
Seuel, P, Albany, N Y.
*Severinghaus, J D,182 Noble st,Chicago,Ills.
*Shaver, Thos A, Irving, Montgom'y co, Ills.
Seyffarth, G, DD, New York City, N Y.
Seyler. T, Derinda Centre, Jo Davies co, Ills.
*Shaffer, J, La Grange, La Grange co, Ind.
*Shaffer, J F, Xenia, Green co, Ohio.
Shaffer, J M, Eve Mills, Monroe co, Tenn.
*Shannon, S G, Milroy, Mifflin co, Pa.
*Sharretts, E A, Fowlersville, Col'a co, Pa.
*Sharts, Wm, Woodstock, Ulster co. N Y.
*Shearer, J F, Bellefontaine. Logan co, Ohio.
*.^heeder, P, New Bloomfield. Perry co Pa.
*Sheeleigh, M, Ed L S S Herald, Whitemarsh,
 Montgomery co, Pa.
Sheely, D, Rockville, Lexington co, S C.
*Shelland, W H, Frey's Bush, Mont'y co, N Y.
Shepperson, W, North Star, Mo.
*Sherer, J F, Shelby, Ohio.
*Sherk, P B, Karthaus, Clearfield co, Pa.
*Sherts, A H, Chambersburg, Frank'n co, Pa.
Sherven, L O, Frenchville,Trempeleau co,Wis.
Shickel, P, Salem, Roanoke co, Va.
Schimmel, C, Toronto, Ont.
*Shindel, Hy C, Port Royal, Juniata co, Pa.
*Shindel, JP, Middleburg, Snyder co, Pa.
*Shindel, M L, Danville, Montour co, Pa.
Shirey, John D, Newberry, S C.
*Shoffner, G F, Somerset, Pa.
*Shoffner, J R, Lionville, Chester co, Pa.
*Shorr, M M, Millersburg, Holmes co, Ohio.
*Short, J, Dongola, Union co, Ills.
*Shoup, J B, Landesburg, Perry co, Pa.
*Shreves, J W, Pottersburg, Union co, Ohio.
Shultes, A, Berne, Albany co, N Y.
*Shultz, James, Avoca, Steuben co, N Y.
Sibert, W M, Howard's Lick, Hardy co,W Va.
Sibole, E E, Salem, Roanoke co, Va.
Sick, Th, ——
*Sickel, Prof B T W, Rutersv'e, Fay'e co, Tex
Siebert, A F, Dayton, Ohio.
Seibke, C H, New Haven, Conn.
*Siechrist, S, New Baltimore, Ohio.
Sieck, J, Patchin, Erie co, N Y.
Sieck, H, Memphis, Tenn.
Siegler, A, Tomah, Monroe co, Wis.
Siegrist, J, Stillwater, Washington co, Minn.
Siek, Th, Champaign City, Ills.
Sieker, J H, St Paul, Minn.
Sievers, F, Frankenlust, Saginaw co, Mich.
Sieving, H, Manito, Mason co, Ills.
Sieving, E A, Lincoln, Benton co, Mo.
Siewers,Prof L, Decorah,Winneshiek co,Iowa.
Sihler, Dr W, Fort Wayne, Ind.
*Sikes, J R, Junction, Rensselaer co, N Y.
Siljestroem, O J, Swede Point, Boone co, Iowa.
*Sill, G, Manchester, Carroll co, Md.
Simon, D, Indiana, Ind co, Pa.
Simonson, J H, Clinton, Rock co, Wis.

Singer, J, New Stanton, Westm'd co, Pa.
*Singley, W H, Springfield, Clark co, Ohio.
*Sinsabaugh, G, St Louisville, Licking co, O.
Sippel, A. Potsdam, Olmsted co, Minn.
Sitzman, E, Terre Haute, Ind.
Sivertsen, H, Benson, Swift co, Minn.
Sjoeblom, P, Red Wing, Goodhue co, Minn.
*Sjoequist, J G, Kerkhaven, Swift co, Minn.
Skeppstedt, A G, Essex, Page co, Iowa.
*Slaybaugh, G H, Lucas, Richland co, Ohio.
Sligh, J A, Frog Level, Newberry co, S C.
*Sloan, W J, Wooster, Wayne co, Ohio.
Smeby, O H, Albert Lea, Freeborn co, Minn.
*Smedley,T S, Sandyville, Tuscarawas co, O.
Smeltzer, J P, DD, Walhalla, Oconee co, S C.
*Smith, A M, Bloomington, Clinton co, Ohio.
*Smith, D, Carthage, Hancock co, Ills.
*Smith, D W, Mansfield, Richland co, Ohio.
Smith. Enoch, Greensburg, Westm'd co, Pa.
*Smith, G H, Columbus, Platte co, Nebraska.
Smith, J H, Wadsworth, Medina co, Ohio.
Smith, J L, Alliance, Stark co, Ohio.
*Smith, J M, Onward, Cass co, Ind.
Smith, J M, Newton, Catawba co, N C.
Smith, O P Z, Trappe, Montgomery co, Pa.
*Smith, P S, Berlin, Mann co, Ohio.
*Smith, R, Gebharts, Somerset co, Pa.
Smith, S R, Matamoras, Montgomery co, Va.
*Smith, S S, Forest, Scott co, Miss.
Smoll, B S, Grimsville, Berks co, Pa.
Snyder, J, Paulding,
*Snyder, S P, Butler, De Kalb co, Ind.
*Snyder, M, Abbottstown, Adams co, Pa.
*Snyder, G W, Cedar Rapids, Iowa.
Snyder, Jos A, N Market, Shenandoah co, Va.
Soeholm, A B J, Perth Amboy, Midd'x co, N J
Soergel, N, St Joseph, Mo.
Soedergren, C H,Porter Station,Porter co, Ind.
Solberg, J P, Primrose, Dane co, Wis.
Solseth, O E, Reesor, Chippewa co, Minn.
Sommer, Dr A, Pittston, Luzerne co, Pa.
Sommer, W M, Long Green, Balt co. Md.
Sommer, J H, 281 Prospect av,Brooklyn, N Y.
Sondhaus, M, Summit, Cook co, Ills.
*Souders, E W, Urbana, Champaign co,Ohio.
Spaeth, Prof A, 1615 Girard av, Phila, Pa.
Spangler, G, Sidney, Shelby co, Ohio.
Spangenberg, Dr J A, Harrisburg, Pa.
Sparks, D, Min'l Point, Tuscarawas co, Ohio.
*Sparr, W M, Fairfield, Jefferson co, Iowa.
Spieker, Prof G F, Kutztown, Berks co, Pa.
Speckhard, Geo, Royal Oak, Oakland co, Mich.
Spehr, O, Sheboygan, Wis.
Spielman, C, Lancaster, Fairfield co, Ohio.
Spindler, F W, Grand Haven, Mich.
*Sprecher, C Spener, Dongola, Union co, Ills.
*Sprecher, D, Richview, Washington co, Ills.
*Sprecher, Prof Isaac, Springfield, Clark co,O.
*Sprecher, Prof S, DD,LLD, Springfield, Ohio.
Sprengeler, C H, Y America, Carver co, Minn.
Sprengeler, H F, Elysian, Le Seuer co, Minn.
Sprengling, I P, Appleton, Outag co, Wis.
Spring, C F, New Hamburg,Waterloo co, Ont.
*Springer, F, DD, Hillsboro', Mont'y co, Ills.
Staiger, P S, Moberly, Randolph co, Mo.
Stahlschmidt, D, Clarence Centre, Erie co.N Y.
*Stail, S, Cobbleskill, Schoharie co. N Y.
*Stamm, P, Marshall, Calhoun co, Mich.
Stampfer, J, Wartburg, Pesth co, Ontario.
Starck, C, Springfield, Ills.
*Startzman, C, Clearspring, Wash'n co, Md.
*Stauffer, Sam'l S, Curllsville, Clarion co, Pa.
Stecher, A D, Potter's Mills, Calumet co,Wis.

Stechholz, H, Martinsville, Niag co, N Y.
*Steck, C T, Altoona, Blair co, Pa.
*Steck, Dan, DD, Middletown, Fred'k co, Md.
*Steck, Jacob, Tiffin, Seneca co, Ohio.
*Steck, J M, Jersey Shore, Lycoming co, Pa.
Steck, Thos, Berwick, Columbia co, Pa.
*Steck, W H, Ardmore, Montgomery co, Pa.
Steege, J H C, Dundee, Kane co, Ills.
Steger, H, Huntington, Ind.
Steen, L, Harrison, Monongalia co, Minn.
Steimle, F W T, 408 Jay st, Brooklyn, N Y.
Steinbach, C F, Fairfield Cen'e, De Kalb, Ind.
Steiner, J M, Rondout, Ulster co, N Y.
*Steinhauer, C, Washington, D C.
*Steininger, J, White Pigeon, St Jos co, Mich.
Steinke, M, Harinsville, Marquette co, Wis.
Steinrauf, W, Huntley, McHenry co, Ills.
*Stelling, G F, DD, Harrisburg, Pa.
Stellhorn, Prof F W, Fort Wayne, Ind.
Stephan, M, Chester, Randolph co, Ills.
Stettler, D M, Beavertown, Snyder co, Pa.
Steup, H C, Morrisania, New York, N Y.
Stibole, E E, Salem, Roanoke co, Va.
Stickley, V, Newport, Giles co, Va.
Stiegemeyer, L, Lyons, Clinton co, Iowa.
Stiling, W C, Stevens Point, Portage co, Wis.
Stirewalt, J N, Stony Man, Page co, Va.
Stirewalt, J P, New Market, Shenan'h co, Va.
Stirewalt, M J, Augusta St'n, Marion co, Ind.
Stockholm, J, ——, Wis.
*Stoever, C F, Mechanicsburg, Cumb'd co, Pa.
*Stock, Daniel, Seven Valley, York co, Pa.
Stock, S F, Fort Wayne, Ind.
Stoeffler, C, Golden Lake, Jefferson co, Wis.
*Stoll, J, Sterling, Whiteside co, Ills.
*Stork, C A, DD, N Paca st, Baltimore, Md.
Storm, F, Collinsville, Madison co, Ills.
*Stough, J H, Knoxville, Marion co, Iowa.
*Stover, M J, Schenectady, N Y.
*Strail, H A, Poestenkill, Rensselaer co, N Y.
Strasberger, E, Cedarburg, Ozaukee co, Wis.
Strasen, C J A, Watertown, Jefferson co, Wis.
*Strauss, A M, Berlin, Somerset co, Pa.
Strauss, C, Okolona, Henry co, Ohio.
Strauss, Wm H, Summit Hill, Carbon co, Pa.
*Streamer, C L, Martinsburg, Blair co, Pa.
Streckfuss, F, Y America, Carver co, Minna.
Streckfusz, J G, Okaw, Washington co, Ills.
Streissguth, W, St Paul, Minn.
Strempfer, J, Wartburg, Pesth co, Ont.
Strieter, J, Proviso, Cook co, Ills.
Strobel, P A, Mt Pleasant, Cabarrus co, N C.
*Strobel, W D, DD, Rhinebeck, Duc'ss co, NY.
Strobel, W T, Wilton, Muscatine co, Iowa.
Stroehlein, G, Glasgow, Howard co, Mo.
*Stroh, N J, Mt Morris, Ogle co, Ills.
*Stroud, C, Springfield, Clarke co, Ohio.
Strodach, H B, Dushore, Sullivan co, Pa.
Stroup, G W, ——, Pa.
Struntz, G A, Mauch Chunk, Carbon, Pa.
Strube, E, Newton, Manitowoc co, Wis.
Stub, H A, Highlandville, Iowa.
Stub, H G, Minneapolis, Minn.
Stubnatzy, W S, Fort Wayne, Ind.
*Stuckenberg, Prof J H W, Springfield, Ohio.
*Studebaker, A H, Colum'a City, Whit'y co, Ind
*Studebaker, E, Franklintown, York co, Pa.
Studt, P, Luzerne, Benton co, Iowa.
Stuerken, C, Baltimore, Md.
Stuecklin, F, Elizabeth City, N J.
Stuelpnagel, M, West Albany, Wab co, Minn.
*Stufft, David, Scalp Level, Cambria co, Pa.
Stuermer, J, Ida Station, Monroe co, Mich.

*Stultz, B F, Albion, Noble co, Ind.
Stumpf, J H, Frostburg, Allegheny co, Md.
Stute, H, Hartland, Shawano co, Wis.
Stutz, G F, Rondout, Ulster co, N Y.
Succop, H H, Sebringville, Perth co, Ontario.
Suel, H G, Minneapolis, Minn.
*Suesserott, B C, Lancaster, Lancaster co, Pa.
Suesz, S, Melvin, Ford co, Ills.
*Suman, J J, 45 First st, Georgetown, D C.
Summers, J, Mechanicstown, Fred'k co, Md.
*Summers, D, St Paris, Champaign co, Ohio.
Sutter, J J, Clyde, Sandusky co, Ohio.
Sutter, G, Versailles, Darke co, Ohio.
Svennungsen, S, Winona, Tremp'n co, Wis.
Sverdrup, Prof G, Minneapolis, Minn.
*Swaney, D D, Nokomis, Montg'y co, Ills.
Swaney, W H, Tarlton, Pickaway co, Ohio.
*Swartz, Joel, DD, Williamsport, Pa.
Sweders, A N, Montana, Boone co, Iowa.
*Sweetzer, E, Saddle River, Bergen co, N J.
*Swick, J W, Ashland, Ashland co, Ohio.
Swingle, S H, Prospect, Butler co, Pa.
Switzer, ——,
*Swope, David, Knowersv'c, Albany co, N Y.

Tackle, J J, Lee, Lee co, Ills.
*Taubner, C M, Ph D, Johnstown, Cam'a co, Pa.
Tegtmyer, Chas, Bremen, Randolph co, Ills.
Telden, F, Toronto, Ontario.
Telleen, J, East Des Moines, Iowa.
Thalberg, ——, Racine, Wis.
Theisz, J G, Madisonville, Hamilton co, Ohio.
Thiel, E, Germania, Marquette co, Wis.
Thiele, G, Burlington, Wis.
*Thoele, W, Pittsfield, Pike co, Ills.
*Thomas, A Z, New Franklin, Stark co, O.
*Thomas, G, PhD, Carbondale, Jack'n co, Ill.
Thomsen, C H, Syracuse, N Y.
Thomsen, N, Neenah, Winnebago co, Wis.
*Thompsen, P, Fort Ridgely, Minn.
Thompson, P, Lac qui Parle, Minn.
*Thompson, Abel N, Schellsburg, Bedf'd co, Pa.
Thompson, W, Owatonna, Steele co, Minn.
Thorsen, J A, Rockdell, Olmstead co, Minn.
Thorsen, M, Martell, Pierce co, Wis.
Thorstensen, K, Siljord, Yellow M co, Minn.
Thorup, C Nilson, Two Rivers, Mor'on co, Minn.
*Thuemmel, C B, DD, Sterling, Whites'e co, Ills.
Thurms, —, Decorah, Winneshiek co, Iowa.
Thurner, J, Guttenberg, Clayton co, Iowa.
Thurow, C, Greenfield, Wis.
Tiemeier, H W, Toledo, Tama co, Iowa.
Tirmenstein, M, New Orleans, La.
Titzel, J R, Zelienople, Butler co, Pa.
*Tjaden, M J, Peoria, Ills.
Tjomsland, Leland, La Salle co, Ills.
Toepel, A, Peshtigo, Oconto co, Wis.
Toewe, M, Arenzville, Cass co, Ills.
Toorup, H A, Hartland, Waukesha co, Wis.
Tornell, A F, Taylor's Falls, Chisago co, Minn.
*Tomlinson, J, Aaronsburg, Centre co, Pa.
*Tomlinson, J A, Ghent, Columbia co, Pa.
Torney, H, Ladington, Mich.
Torgersen, T A, Bristol, Worth co, Iowa.
Torgersen, O E, Wissner, Neb.
Torgersen, J Z, 182 N Peoria st, Chicago, Ills.
Tornquist, F A, Attica, Fountain co, Ind.
*Townsend, D, N Bethlehem, Clarion co, Pa
Trabert, Geo H, Elizabetht'n, Lancaster co, Pa.
Tramm, F R, Vincennes, Knox co, Ind.
Traub, G, Crete, Will co, Ind.
Traub, L G, Grant, Kankakee co, Ills.
Trauger, J L, Manor Station, Westm'd co, Pa.

www.ingramcontent.com/pod-product-compliance
Lightning Source LLC
Chambersburg PA
CBHW021436090426
42739CB00009B/1505